Fernando Molina received his A.B. degree from Harvard where he majored in philosophy, studying under Willard V. O. Quine and C. I. Lewis. After graduation and two years with the U. S. Marine Corps, he resumed studies at Yale under such scholars as Brand Blanshard and Arthur Pap. He received his Ph.D. from Yale in 1959 and has since then been on the faculty of the Department of Philosophy at Syracuse University.

EXISTENTIALISM
As Philosophy

Fernando Molina

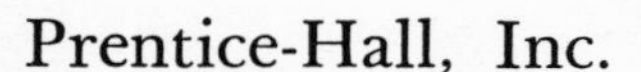

Prentice-Hall, Inc. *Englewood Cliffs, N.J.*

Library of Congress Catalog Card No.: 62-13727
Printed in the United States of America

29426-C

To
Arlene

Preface

One of the many circumstances which occasioned the writing of this book was my hearing an excellent paper on Edmund Husserl's phenomenology delivered by Maurice Natanson at the meeting of the American Philosophical Association in December 1959. Afterward, I wrote to Professor Natanson; he promptly replied. The upshot of this and subsequent correspondence was my coming to see for the first time the intimate relationship that exists between contemporary existentialism and Husserlian phenomenology. The closeness of this relationship has made it possible for the insights of Sören Kierkegaard and Friedrich Nietzsche to be absorbed into a type of philosophizing as well-defined and as formidable as any that has engaged the minds of the West.

Among individuals deserving my thanks are Professors Herbert Spiegelberg of Lawrence College and James Edie of Northwestern: exchanges of ideas and materials with them have helped crystallize and clarify my own thinking on existentialism and phenomenology. Mr. Camilo Gonzales and Mrs. Debra Bergoffen (née Hantman) provided me with valuable materials. Mrs. Martha Husain's assistance was especially helpful in my struggles to decipher the cryptic content of Martin Heidegger's *Sein und Zeit*. She combined her knowledge of German and her fine talent for philosophy to produce a set of notes that helped me find my way to and through some of the more forbidding passages in Heidegger. I am also indebted to Professor C. G. Christofides of Syracuse University for help on the French of Sartre.

My thanks also go to Bruce Bowen of Prentice-Hall, Inc., for indicating the need for this book, and to Richard W. Hansen, vice-president of Prentice-Hall, for taking the time and trouble to discuss the project with me while it was still just a noble intent.

I especially wish to thank my wife, Arlene, for reasons too numerous to list.

Fernando Molina

Acknowledgments

The author gratefully acknowledges permission to quote from the following publishers: George Allen & Unwin Ltd. (Nietzsche's *The Will to Power*); Farrar, Straus & Cudahy, Inc. (Sartre's *The Transcendence of the Ego*); The New American Library of World Literature, Inc. (Trocchi's *The Outsiders*); The Macmillan Company, New York (Edmund Husserl's *Ideas.* Copyright 1952 by Allen & Unwin, London); Oxford University Press (Tolstoy's *The Death of Iván Ilých*); The Clarendon Press, Oxford (*The Logic of Hegel* and Hegel's *Philosophy of Mind*); Philosophical Library, Inc. (Sartre's *The Psychology of the Imagination* and *Being and Nothingness*); The Viking Press, Inc. (Kaufmann's *The Portable Nietzsche*); Random House, Inc. (*The Philosophy of Nietzsche,* translated by Clifton Fadiman); N. V. Martinus Nijhoff's (Husserl's *Cartesian Meditations*); Max Niemeyer Verlag (9th Edition of Heidegger's *Sein und Zeit*); Princeton University Press (Kierkegaard's *Concluding Unscientific Postscript* and *The Concept of Dread*); Librairie Gallimard (Sartre's *L'Être et le néant*); Henry Regnery Company (Nietzsche's *Beyond Good and Evil*).

Table of Contents

Introduction

. . . when it is a question of existential concepts it always is a sign of surer tact to abstain from definitions, because one does not like to construe in the form of a definition which so easily makes something else and something different out of a thought which essentially must be understood in a different fashion and which one has understood differently and has loved in an entirely different way.

SÖREN KIERKEGAARD, The Concept of Dread

I

In his now classic "Existentialism Is a Humanism," Jean-Paul Sartre states that existentialism is a philosophy for technicians and philosophers. Seldom in the history of thought has so authoritative a statement been so widely disregarded. Many people who take a genuine interest in the history of ideas continue to look on existentialism as merely a philosophy of the cafés, a highly imaginative rationalization of human misery assuming the guise of sophistication.

To deplore this one-sided yet popular conception of existentialism is not to deny that there are themes in existentialism which lend themselves to pseudo-philosophical and often loose treatment. The existential themes of death, dread, and bad-faith, for example, receive such treatment, not so much owing to the absence or inadequacy of the logic employed by those dealing with them, but rather to a common misunderstanding of what the existentialists—Martin Heidegger and Jean-Paul Sartre in particular—are attempting to do. One of the main purposes of this study is to help correct this misunderstanding and to exhibit existentialism as a technical philosophy.

To effect this reinterpretation of existentialism it must be established that Heidegger and Sartre deal with existential themes within a technical philosophical framework. The *form* which this framework imposes on the *thematic material* removes the treatment of such concepts as death and dread from the realm of popular discourse and places them in the realm of a technical philosophical methodology. I propose in this study (a) to state the central problems and themes of existentialism, the *substance;* (b) to explicate the framework within which those themes are to be developed, the *form*; and (c) to illustrate by an examination of Heidegger and Sartre the synthesis of *substance* and *form.*

II

It is not easy to define existentialism; moreover, it is probably impossible to provide a definition with which all students and members of the existentialist movement would agree. A difficulty in defining the term is that any definition given is of necessity after the fact. In other words, anyone defining existentialism has to deal with the matter-of-fact situation that a certain group of individuals *are* existentialists; that is, certain thinkers are considered to be existentialists, even though they show no one common characteristic that might conceivably be taken as essential to the philosophy of existence.

My own definition—perhaps better termed a characterization—centers on two aspects significant and widespread among those men, both academic philosophers and men of letters, who are considered existentialists. I define existentialism as a type of philosophizing which endeavors to analyze the basic structures of human existence and to call individuals to an awareness of their existence in its essential freedom.

One immediate consequence of a reference to the "essential freedom" of human existence in this characterization of existentialism is that two of the figures who have most influenced the course of contemporary existentialism, and who have on occasion been classified as existentialists, are not by my definition to be considered true members of the movement at all. Nietzsche explicitly denies human freedom; Husserl indicates no major concern with the concept of human freedom and exhibits a genuine—if philosophical!—distaste for the "concrete worldly existence" of man.

However, the refusal to classify either Nietzsche or Husserl as existentialists does not constitute a denial of their relevance to the philosophy of existence as it has in fact taken shape. Distinction between the *problems* and the *themes* of existentialism may indicate that Nietzsche, in his rejection of human freedom and his downgrading of the role of consciousness, does not answer certain problems in a manner that would lead to our considering him an existentialist. Yet many of the *themes* sounded by Nietzsche have become integral aspects of existentialist thought, as, for example, in the reflections of Heidegger and Sartre. Prominent examples of Nietzschean themes later integrated into existentialism are the death of God, the nonexistence of an "other" world, and the fact of human responsibility for all value systems. Husserl has had so great an influence on the later existentialists that often theses developed by them can be read and understood only after acquaintance with Husserl's phenomenology. The Husserlian background is all-important in several cases, particularly in reading Sartre.

III

In this study I have not attempted to give a comprehensive view of the position of any one thinker simply for the sake of complete coverage. In fact, in order to present *existentialism,* rather than the *existentialists,* I have purposely chosen and developed only those figures and topics which illustrate the systematic unity of existentialistic thought. This selectivity obtains particularly in the case of Nietzsche; a longer discussion of him would have provided a better look at the richness of his thought, but would not have furthered appreciably the understanding of existentialism.

It might also be noted that my treatment of Hegel is colored by similar considerations: the need not so much for an understanding of Hegel as for an illumination of Kierkegaard's conception of Hegel. Although a more sympathetic presentation of Hegel's position could have been made, it might not have thrown so much light on Kierkegaard's tortured dialectics.

By the same token, in dealing with Kierkegaard the usual emphasis on becoming a Christian has been subordinated to emphasis on becoming subjective. Existentialism would be a lesser mode of thought and Kierkegaard a smaller figure if the philosophy and the man had no relevance beyond a Christian (religious or theological) domain. Some of Heidegger's thoughts, on conscience and guilt, for example, have suffered a similar confinement, but for a different reason. His analyses of the essential structures of human existence are too significant for the future development of philosophy to be clouded by a swarm of nonessential quasi-theological details.

This study is not intended to be comprehensive; many important figures have not been mentioned in it. The outstanding omission is without doubt Maurice Merleau-Ponty; later historians of philosophy may rank him above Sartre as an exponent of phenomenological existentialism, although Sartre's present international stature is undeniable. More background could have been presented; I have in mind especially a discussion of Pascal's *Pensées*. However, I consider that a treatment of Kierkegaard and Nietzsche meets the basic requirement for the kind of understanding that only the historical approach can provide, insofar as the historical background of existentialism has undeniably helped to shape its present form.

IV

I have tried to present the *heart* of existentialism, the technical core constituted by the actual descriptions made by existentialists of the essential structures of human existence. This aspect of the philosophy of existence has not received sufficient consideration. The contribution of existentialism as the substantial, often technical, philosophy that it is cannot be overstressed; its proper place is as one other stage in the development of Western philosophy.

Unless existentialism is accepted as one mode of philosophizing among others, and unless it is debated without prejudice in that capacity, we are, I suggest, wrongly condemning it to the role of a modern aestheticism—a seeking for pseudo-philosophical excitement in a world where all excitement serves merely to fill in the time before death. Admittedly there may be need for excitement in a world in which the ultimate alternative, not *how to live* but *how to die,* is scarcely any longer a matter of choice. Yet existentialism deprived of its technical philosophical core is nihilism wearing the mask either of the café or of the lecture platform: a mere mask—albeit perhaps a convincing one. To such a despairing conception of existentialism there is an alternative, which this study is intended to illustrate: *Existentialism is the systematic, often technical, exploration of the category of the individual.*

Kierkegaard: The Category of the Individual

1

The individual is the category through which . . . this age, all history, the human race as a whole, must pass.

SÖREN KIERKEGAARD, The Point of View

More than one hundred years ago, the Danish philosopher and theologian Sören Kierkegaard asserted, somewhat cryptically, that *truth is subjectivity*. Whatever debate has since arisen as to what Kierkegaard intended by this statement, the extent to which its presumed meaning has been influential in determining the form of contemporary existentialism is above argument. Furthermore, I suggest that the statement, if viewed against the intellectual background of the time in which it was set down, is clear and unambiguous in its meaning.

The intellectual background in question is the all-encompassing philosophical system of the German philosopher G. W. F. Hegel, which, as Walter Lowrie has indicated in his classic study, *Kierkegaard,* dominated the thinking of the intellectual youth of Copenhagen at that time, a group of which Kierkegaard was a member.[1] For the moment then, we shall concern ourselves with the notions of truth and subjectivity as they were developed by Hegel, viewing them as a point of departure for understanding Kierkegaard's statement that truth is subjectivity. Of truth Hegel says:

> In common life truth means the agreement of an object with our conception of it. We thus presuppose an object to which our conception

[1] Walter Lowrie, *Kierkegaard* (London: Oxford University Press, 1938), p. 78.

> must conform. In the philosophical sense of the word, on the other hand, truth may be described, in general abstract terms, as the agreement of a thought-content with itself. This meaning is quite different from the one given above. At the same time the deeper and philosophical meaning of truth can be partially traced even in the ordinary usage of language. Thus we speak of a true friend; by which we mean a friend whose manner of conduct accords with the notion of friendship. In the same way we speak of a true work of art. Untrue in this sense means the same as bad, or self-discordant. In this sense a bad state is an untrue state; and evil and untruth may be said to consist in the contradiction subsisting between the function or notion and the existence of the object.[2]

In this passage from Hegel's *Logic,* the point to be noted as relevant to an understanding of Kierkegaard is the somewhat peculiar meaning which Hegel gives to the concept of truth. The definition of truth proposed by Hegel differs from that generally accepted by such modern philosophers as Bertrand Russell, for whom truth was once a correspondence between belief and fact.[3] On the basis of the passage cited above, it appears that truth for Hegel is an *ontological* notion; that is, truth is "in the ordinary usage of language" something ascribed to a *thing,* rather than to a belief or a sentence or proposition. For Hegel, a thing is true if its character is in accordance with its notion, its essence or function. A *true* soldier is a man who is a soldier in the fullest sense possible; that is, he exhibits in his professional life all the virtues of a military man; his conduct *is in accordance with* the essence of soldiering. Moreover, and by way of making the transition from the adjective "true" to the noun "truth," we can speak of the *truth* of an individual as *the state of being in accord with* the essence of individuality, with what an individual *ought to be.*

In view of this analysis of Hegel's notion of truth, we can now partially clarify Kierkegaard's statement that truth is subjectivity by stating it in a less truncated form: the truth of the existing individual is in accordance with the notion of subjectivity.[4]

[2] G. W. F. Hegel, *The Logic of Hegel,* trans. Wallace (London: Oxford University Press, 1950), pp. 51-52.

[3] Bertrand Russell, *The Problems of Philosophy* (New York: Oxford University Press, 1959), p. 123.

[4] The interpretation of this point opposes that of Walter Kaufmann. Cf. Kaufmann's *From Shakespeare to Existentialism* (New York: Doubleday & Company, Inc., 1960), p. 193 ff.

To this notion of subjectivity we now turn our attention, first examining Hegel's views on a related problem, the nature of the self:

> By the term "I" I mean myself, a single and altogether determinate person. And yet I really utter nothing peculiar to myself, for every one else is an "I" or "Ego," and when I call myself "I," though I indubitably mean the single person myself, I express a thorough universal. "I," therefore, is mere being-for-self, in which everything peculiar or marked is renounced and buried out of sight; it is as it were the ultimate and unanalyzable point of consciousness. We may say [that] "I" and thought are the same, or, more definitely, [that] "I" is thought as a thinker.[5]

The significance of this passage to the present discussion can best be seen by raising the question of what, for Hegel, is the truth of the self; what character ought the self to have if it is to be in accord with its notion? The answer is not difficult to obtain; this passage leaves little doubt that the "I," the self, is *thought*. The *"I"* is conceived by Hegel to be a thinker. The existing person is identified with the thought.

The comparison of Hegel's conception of the self with Kierkegaard's approach to the problem of subjectivity is stated clearly and forcefully by Kierkegaard himself:

> The systematic Idea [of Hegel's] is the identity of subject and object, the unity of thought and being. Existence, on the other hand, is their separation. It does not by any means follow that existence is thoughtless; but it has brought about, and brings about, a separation between subject and object, thought and being.[6]

What purpose is served by this insistence on the separation of subject and object in (human) existence? Kierkegaard, in his answer to this question, rightly points out that for Hegel the thought in question is not *someone's thought,* but pure thought, thought in itself. Yet the self *is* the thought; and this self is, as seen in the last passage cited from Hegel, itself a universal thinker *in general, not* a particular thinker. It is then easy to see why Kierkegaard is troubled by the fact that for Hegel "the existing subjectivity tends

[5] Hegel, *Logic,* p. 48.

[6] Sören Kierkegaard, *Concluding Unscientific Postscript,* trans. Swenson (Princeton, N. J.: Princeton University Press, 1944), p. 112. This reference hereafter cited as *CUP*.

more and more to evaporate."[7] Whatever else may be at stake, Kierkegaard's main point here is certainly an insistence on the primacy of the subject, a subject who may or may not think but who certainly exists:

> The existing subject . . . is engaged in existing, which is indeed the case with every human being.[8]

In pointing up the contrast between Hegel and Kierkegaard on the truth of the individual, it is important not to overstate the case against Hegel in order to delineate Kierkegaard's conception of subjectivity. Rather, to see what, besides thought, the individual may possess according to Hegel, is to enable oneself to see the significant difference between him and Kierkegaard. My point is not that Hegel does not admit into the concept of the individual *subjective elements* such as volition and freedom, but that Hegel denies the *subjectivity* of the individual, if only by omission.

The relation that holds, according to Hegel, between the "I" and the subjective elements of the individual is illustrated in this short passage:

> What I have in my consciousness, is for me. "I" is the vacuum or receptacle for anything and everything: for which everything is and which stores up everything in itself. Every man is a whole world of conceptions, that lie buried in the night of the "Ego." . . . it [the "Ego"] is not a mere universality and nothing more, but the universality which includes in it everything.[9]

In the earlier examination of Hegel's views on the self, the self as thought is a universal, the same for different individuals. In the passage just cited, the relation between the self, a universal, and the particulars that constitute it is described by Hegel by means of the repeated use of metaphors of *containment:* the "I" is a *vacuum* or *receptacle,* it *stores* up things in itself, and these things are *buried,* and *included in* it. I submit that these metaphors of containment are not merely accidentally chosen by Hegel, but are related bits of evidence that Hegel is viewing the individual by means of objective categories; that is, by means of general ideas borrowed from

[7] *CUP,* p. 112.
[8] *CUP,* p. 112.
[9] Hegel, *Logic,* p. 48.

the world of *things* and *events* instead of the world of persons. But only persons may be subjects, may have subjectivity; it is to an awareness of one's own subjectivity that Kierkegaard would have us direct our attention.

There is also an element missing in Hegel's viewpoint. Is the self, for example *your* self, essentially a thinking being? Is a self primarily a *container* of various thoughts and feelings? If these questions can be answered negatively, Hegel's analysis of the self has somehow "left something out." My own use of metaphor here has to be clarified, for, in a sense, no-thing has been "left out" of the analysis. The Hegelian analysis cannot be completed by pointing to some other factor, there for inspection, needing only to be included in the formula of the self.

On the contrary, what has been "left out," subjectivity, could not possibly have been included, given Hegel's mode of approach to the problem at hand. A strange question may clarify what is meant by Hegel's "mode of approach." How could we characterize a situation in which a blind person were to serve as judge in a photography contest? The answer to this question must explain the obvious absurdity involved in trying to conceive of a blind person as judge of photographs; the answer must demonstrate in a logically forceful manner why the situation in question is absurd. Certainly the answer would be that the categories with respect to which a photograph is judged are visual categories; for example, contrasts of shades, balance of parts, unity of impression. Indeed, the pictures themselves are visual objects. We would say, then, that the categories with respect to which a blind person can make a judgment are simply not adequate to the task of judging visual objects; the blind person's *mode of approach* is such that he can never encounter the object which, in such a contest, he would be called upon to judge.

Thus Hegel approaches the analysis of the self with categories such as those with which he would analyze an object or event. But can the self be so approached? Is it a universal that somehow encloses or contains within itself a set of particulars? Or would it be less misleading to speak of the self as *living in* its particulars? Or, perhaps even better, as *unfolding itself* by means of its particulars?

A problem that these questions are intended to illustrate centers around the virtual impossibility of avoiding the use of metaphor in any attempt to discuss the self. In philosophy, especially in those areas of contemporary philosophy in which the meaningfulness of an assertion is held to be dependent upon its empirical confirmability, the use of metaphor is actively discouraged in favor of the literal employment of language. Language literally employed, however, is singularly ill-suited to deal with human subjectivity; it tends to *objectify* that portion of the world about which discourse is taking place. And, when we are seeking to describe a world of *subjects* rather than objects and events, objectification is tantamount to mutilation or destruction.

In brief, to the question, "What is subjectivity," there is no literal answer. Any hints, descriptions, explanations, or definitions can, at best, serve (1) to clarify what subjectivity is not, (2) to illustrate figuratively what some of its aspects are, and (3) to orient the questioner towards what might enable him to become aware of his own subjectivity. Clarification of what the subject is not we shall postpone until the discussion of Sartre, for whom the self is nothing; Sartre's paradoxical use of the word "nothing" will then also be examined. Our attention has been engaged in this chapter, as it will be again in Chapters 1 and 4, on the figurative illustration of some of the aspects of subjectivity. The third objective, to bring about an awareness of subjectivity on the part of the individuals in his audience, is one to which Kierkegaard devoted much of his intellectual energy. Since, as noted above, it is virtually impossible to speak *literally* about human existence, Kierkegaard, to make his readers aware of existence, usually employed indirect communication; that is, he used such forms as journal, pseudo-diary, fiction, and religious polemic and commentary. Whereas in direct communication the importance lies in the objective truth which is communicated without regard for the manner of its reception, in indirect communication the emphasis is placed on the manner in which the thought is appropriated—received into the reader's subjectivity. For further illustration of the technique of indirect communication, the reader is referred to the works of Kierkegaard themselves, since the task of bringing about an awareness of existence is not a proper part of this study, which is a survey of certain aspects of existentialism rather than itself an existential essay.

According to Kierkegaard, not only is subjectivity the essence of man, but freedom and the responsibility that goes with it are the essence of subjectivity. This primacy of freedom in Kierkegaard's thinking is no doubt responsible for some of his exaggerations regarding it, exaggerations whose echoes are still found in Sartre. But the significance which this concept has for Kierkegaard can be put in an interesting perspective by again looking at Hegel. For

Hegel, freedom is an attribute reserved ultimately only for God. Although Hegel writes that individuals achieve freedom by virtue of their participation in the state, a closer look at the *precise* meaning that this concept of human freedom has for Hegel reveals the meaninglessness of the concept. This meaninglessness of freedom, when freedom is attributed to individuals living in a state, stems from the fact that the freedom in question is defined by Hegel as the submission of the will of man to the will of God, for Hegel believed that the will of God takes the form of law in a state or nation.[10] God's will, manifested as the laws or *spirit* of a nation, is particularized, is *ingredient* in persons, but Hegel unambiguously states that it entirely dominates these persons from within. The individuals composing a nation take this spirit—which appears to them in the guise of a personal aim—as their true being.

> Thus, without any selective reflection, the person performs its duty as *his own* and as something which *is;* and in this necessity *he* has himself and his actual freedom.[11]

Thus in Hegel's conception of the ethical, one is free precisely when one is really not free. It is to thinking of this type that Kierkegaard's conception of the individual and of the ethical is a reply.

First, in speaking of the individual, Hegel had disclaimed knowledge whose aim was to detect the peculiarities and passions of men, which would ". . . lay bare what are called the recesses of the human heart." He continues:

> Information of this kind is, for one thing, meaningless, unless on the assumption that we know the *universal*—man as man, and, that always must be, as mind.[12]

We have already seen that Kierkegaard rejects this definition of man as essentially mind; he especially rejects Hegel's emphasis on what is universal in man, thereby giving preference to the existing individual:

> . . . for my task was as a humble servant . . . to provoke, if possible, to invite, to stir up the many to press through this defile of "the individid-

[10] Hegel, *Selections,* ed. J. Loewenberg (New York: Charles Scribner's Sons, 1929), p. 387.

[11] Hegel, *Philosophy of Mind,* trans. Wallace (Oxford: The Clarendon Press, 1894), pp. 119-120.

[12] Hegel, *Philosophy of Mind,* p. 3.

ual," through which, however, no one can pass except by becoming the individual. . . .[13]

Second, regarding the ethical, Kierkegaard bluntly states his opposition to the Hegelian misallocation of responsibility: the ethical makes everyone ". . . responsible for the use to which he puts his life. . . ." [14] Unlike the Hegelian, whose thought addresses itself to man in general, Kierkegaard chooses to remind us that we exist as particular men; and in contrast to Hegel's belief that individuals perform their duty because of the controlling immanence of God's will, Kierkegaard maintains that the individual's ethical reality is exclusively his own, realizable only by him.

For Kierkegaard, ethics is a task in which the individual neither receives help from the "world-historical" nor concerns himself with it, the term "world-historical" being Hegel's means of referring to those individuals whom God employs in shaping the course of history because of their sense for the "ripeness of the times." Kierkegaard's ethical individual is an individual concerned inwardly with his spirit, not with the course of universal history.[15] He sees in ethics the highest task encountered by a human being, the task of becoming subjective, of achieving the truth of man.[16]

Of central importance to the task of becoming subjective is the realization of decisiveness.[17] Although there is no decisiveness without subjectivity, neither can there be subjectivity without decisiveness. Hegel, on the other hand, by defining man as essentially rational rather than subjective, effectively eliminated human freedom from his world view. He was therefore unable to give proper weight to the factor of decisiveness in the makeup of the person.

The decisiveness that is rooted in subjectivity is not a *mere* decisiveness for Kierkegaard, however; there is a matter of *interest,* of passionate involvement respecting one's death, one's eternal happiness after death, and one's very existence.[18] The contemplative individual, the *purely* objective individual, neither feels the need for decision nor sees decision anywhere.[19] But for the subjective

[13] Sören Kierkegaard, *The Point of View, etc.,* trans. Lowrie (London: Oxford University Press, 1939), pp. 130-131.

[14] *CUP,* p. 307, footnote.

[15] *CUP,* p. 128.

[16] *CUP,* p. 119.

[17] *CUP,* p. 33.

[18] *CUP,* p. 51, p. 148; see especially p. 279.

[19] *CUP,* pp. 34-35.

Jeanie -

Please put these in your suitcase for Dr. Pickett.

thank you -

individual, an Abraham, for example, even the fact of a revelation involves that individual in a process of unending reflection regarding the source, the meaning, and the validity of the revelation. The point is that a revelation in itself settles nothing, and reflection, if unlimited by decisiveness, goes on endlessly and fruitlessly.[20] Sartre has cogently restated this belief for our own century by declaring that, from the point of view of existentialism, not even the existence of God would make a difference to a responsibly decisive individual:[21]

> . . . man himself interprets the sign as he chooses.[22]

But decisiveness, even when passionate, still does not fully constitute the subject, for there remains the possibility that the subject's decisiveness might be exercised sporadically. One needs personal continuity, and such continuity, for Kierkegaard, is not a mere fact but an *achievement* on the part of subjectivity. This achievement requires that the individual not only arrive at a decision regarding a project, but also that he renew that decision to pursue the project.

This need for renewal of one's decisions obviously presents problems which we all recognize independently of any acquaintance with existentialism. But for Kierkegaard the role of this need attains heroic proportions because of the very fact *that* the need has to be met in order for the subject to attain personal continuity. Differently stated, there is no personal continuity *already there* to guarantee or even to aid the renewal of a decision. Thus a renewal can only be approached in dread. The recurrent emphasis in existentialism on the mood of dread or anxiety stems from just this absence of personal continuity, for the subject who seeks to constitute his personal continuity by renewal of a decision does so as a free individual, but free *in two different respects.* On the one hand, he is free in that he is *self-determined;* the choice and the would-be renewal of it are acts for which he alone is responsible. But, on the other hand, he is also free in that he is *indeterminate;* prior to his successful renewal of decision, there is no continuity, no fixity of self, to see him *with certainty* through the act of renewal of choice and

[20] *CUP,* p. 35, footnote.

[21] Jean-Paul Sartre, "Existentialism Is a Humanism," *Existentialism from Dostoevsky to Sartre,* ed. Kaufmann (New York: Meridian Books, The World Publishing Company, 1951), p. 311.

[22] Sartre, "Existentialism Is a Humanism," p. 295.

pursuit of the original project. An individual who sees that his freedom—his choices—in the future is not now guaranteed enters a state of anxiety.[23] The concept of anxiety, which has achieved such prominence in many commentaries and discussions of existentialism, is undeniably important to the structure of existentialistic thinking, but too emphatic a discussion of anxiety tends to detract from what, I would suggest, is by far the more fundamental point. This basic realization, appearing in Kierkegaard and reaching its culmination in Sartre, permits freedom to be at once the *essential* characteristic of man yet not a *defining* or *delimiting* characteristic. Freedom is determinate as a *source* of spontaneity, yet it is indeterminate with respect to the *direction* that the exercise of spontaneity will take. Finally, and most important, freedom is not something we *have;* it is something we *are*.

Kierkegaard's commitment to so extreme a conception of human freedom, although developed explicitly in his *The Concept of Dread,* appears implicitly throughout the massive *Concluding Unscientific Postscript* in the many references to the *becoming* of the subject in time:

> The principle that the existing subjective thinker is constantly occupied in striving, does not mean that he has . . . a goal toward which he strives, and that he would be finished when he had reached this goal. No, he strives infinitely, *is constantly in process of becoming.*[24]

Existence is a striving in time, a *venture*. Our task is not only to become subjective and to achieve the personal continuity of our subjectivity; it is also, for Kierkegaard, to *become* a Christian, a task made difficult by the paradoxical nature of the Christian truth, the appearance of an *eternal* God in the *historical* person of the Christ.

Too many discussions of this aspect of Kierkegaard's thinking, it seems to me, have been vitiated not by overemphasis placed on the task of becoming a Christian, but rather by underemphasis of Kierkegaard's insight here—an insight which obtains, to put it frankly, whether or not one is a Christian, and even whether or not one is religious at all. In Kierkegaard's position regarding the Christian paradox, especially as it relates to the significance of *the instant* (to

[23] Sören Kierkegaard, *The Concept of Dread,* trans. Lowrie (Princeton, N. J.: Princeton University Press, 1957), pp. 38-40, 55, 99-100.

[24] *CUP,* p. 84. Italics mine.

be contrasted with *the moment* in the discussion that follows), there is a real contribution to philosophical thinking about the nature of time and time-consciousness, a contribution as valuable as those advanced by Kant and Bergson.

Stated first only in its specifically Christian guise, Kierkegaard's thesis is that the truth of Christianity which the existing subject must appropriate and then renew is, logically, an absurdity; for how can God, an *eternal* being, make an appearance in *time* in the person of the Christ? [25] How much of the substance of Christianity rests on the fact of there being meaningful relatedness between God in heaven, the eternal, and the Christ and men on earth, the temporal? But how can this relatedness possibly be conceived? For Kierkegaard it cannot, and in that fact rests the absurdity of Christianity:

> In my God-relationship I have to learn precisely to give up my finite understanding. . . .[26]

Kierkegaard's interest in the absurdity of Christianity lies strongly in the consideration that, if Christianity is absurd, then the truth of Christianity remains objectively uncertain. This uncertainty regarding the objective truth of Christianity makes faith (as contrasted with knowledge) possible, for without the element of risk in believing what is uncertain, there can be no faith.[27]

This statement of Kierkegaard's irrationalism indicates the questionable nature of a faith, the very meaning of which is absurd to human reason. I suggest, however, that the genuinely philosophical issue with which Kierkegaard is dealing here, an issue that continues to merit study, is his concern with the absurdity of Christianity *not* in its relation to the possibility of faith, but rather in its relation to the problem of human time-awareness. This problem concerns the human awareness of a particular moment as having a significance that transcends the moment in question. This point can be developed by illustrating the difference between a *moment* and what Kierkegaard calls an *instant*.[28] In philosophy we often make the distinction between physical time, on the one hand, and

[25] *CUP,* p. 188.
[26] *CUP,* p. 159.
[27] *CUP,* p. 182.
[28] What follows includes of necessity a great deal of interpretation of some often unclear points made by Kierkegaard in *The Concept of Dread,* pp. 73-83.

psychological time, on the other. Physical time refers to the flow of events in nature considered without regard to the presence or experience of an observer; this is the time measured by clocks of whatever kind. Psychological time, on the contrary, is the time of the flux of one's experience. It is the time which passes quickly when we are happily engaged in an agreeable task, and slowly when our circumstances are not of so pleasant a nature. We can say of both of these types of time, physical and psychological, that they are composed of moments, units of time each capable of being viewed in and by itself.

Disregarding physical time, we can say that units of psychological time are not always capable of being exhaustively described if they are treated merely as self-contained units; some of them have the *significance* which qualifies them as *instants* in the generalized Kierkegaardian sense suggested here.[29] The moment of insight into a law of the universe by a Newton or an Einstein illustrates the difference between a moment and an instant.[30] Many moments may pass in the reflective life of a thinker, some slowly, some quickly. Then at one point in his reflection the person reflecting may *see* that a certain principle regarding the nature of the universe is true, or at least highly possible, on the basis of his reflections. This insight has taken place at one moment, but that moment, in virtue of the insight, is transformed, is different in a striking way from the moments that preceded it. For in that moment a truth about the universe, timeless in itself, has made its appearance, not just in the experience but in the understanding of an individual existing essentially, as Kierkegaard would say, *in time*. That moment of insight constitutes itself as an *instant* in virtue of its being not just "an atom of time," but also "an atom of eternity":

> Such a moment has a peculiar character. It is brief and temporal indeed, like every moment; it is transient as all moments are; it is past, like every moment in the next moment. And yet it is decisive, and filled with the eternal. Such a moment ought to have a distinctive name; let us call it the *Fullness of Time*.[31]

[29] Only the extreme case is being illustrated here; it may be that in human consciousness all or nearly all moments are instants.

[30] Cf. José Ortega y Gasset, *What Is Philosophy?* (New York: W. W. Norton & Company, Inc., 1961), p. 21 ff.

[31] Sören Kierkegaard, "Philosophical Fragments," *A Kierkegaard Anthology*, ed. Bretall (New York: The Modern Library, Random House, 1946), p. 161.

For Kierkegaard the instant is the moment of apprehending the truth of Christianity. But if, as has already been noted, the truth of Christianity is an absurdity, how then can the individual *truly* become a Christian, Kierkegaard's notion of the instant notwithstanding? The answer to this question brings together two of Kierkegaard's main theses in a somewhat unusual fashion. For, if *the truth of man is subjectivity,* inwardness, then the individual seeking to become a Christian has to maximize his inwardness. But what better means, for Kierkegaard, can there be for maximizing one's inwardness than by being passionately concerned with truth of Christianity *if only because the absurdity, and therefore the uncertainty,* of Christianity call for passionate concern in the absence of an objectively attainable truth?

> Without [an intellectual] risk [regarding the objective truth of one's beliefs] there is no faith. Faith is precisely the contradiction between the infinite passion of the individual's inwardness and the objective uncertainty.[32]

Thus Kierkegaard's approach to the paradox that is Christianity itself culminates in a paradox; for if the individual is in the right God-relationship, in the proper state of intensified inwardness, he is *in truth* even if the object to which he is so related (the Incarnation) be itself false.[33]

This awkward conclusion on Kierkegaard's part (which has been the occasion for much well-deserved criticism of him) reflects a tension in Kierkegaard's thinking. He sometimes keeps the two main aspects of his thought apart; but at other times, as in his conclusion just noted above, they are merged with not always happy results. These two aspects, unless one's attention is carefully focused upon them, are easy to confuse with each other, and Kierkegaard's failure to keep them separated, or at least *explicitly interrelated,* is understandable. The two aspects in question are, first, the concern with awakening his audience to the true meaning of existence, subjectivity, and second, the concern with identifying the process of becoming a Christian with a certain mode of existence rather than with the purely formal acceptance of a certain set of "beliefs." Insofar as the task of achieving the true meaning of existence involves an em-

[32] *CUP,* p. 182.
[33] *CUP,* p. 178.

phasis on responsibility, decisiveness, passionate involvement, and risk, it is not unreasonable to grant that only an individual whose existence fully exhibits these characteristics could be said to be capable of truly becoming a Christian. But if the truth of Christianity is an absurdity and thereby unjustifiable, it is not reasonable to assert the reverse of this last point; namely, that only by becoming, or seeking to become, a true Christian can one achieve the richest possible existence. That the absurdity of Christianity makes the process of becoming a Christian a risky venture is true, to be sure; but so also are other tasks whose demands upon us are not without rational meaning or evidence.

My point here is that Kierkegaard's personal commitment to a form of Christianity for which no justification can be asked, although perhaps the dominant aspect of his thinking, reveals an unfortunately antirationalistic fact about Kierkegaard, the person. It is not, however, his essential contribution to existentialism, if by existentialism we mean responsible philosophizing regarding the truth of human existence. Kierkegaard contributes significantly to the development of existentialism when he addresses himself to his age, an age which has forgotten what inwardness signifies and what it means to exist.[34] Nowhere is this forgetfulness of existence more easy to see than in the behavior of a crowd, which, as Kierkegaard is quick to see and underscore, is really the behavior of *each individual* in the crowd:

> For "Crowd" is an abstraction and has no hands; but each individual has ordinarily two hands, and so when an individual lays his two hands on Caius Marius [an ancient Roman whose life was once spared when no one of his captors could steel himself to carry out the group's death decree; cf. Plutarch's *Lives*] they are the two hands of the individual, certainly not those of his neighbor, and still less those of the . . . crowd which has no hands.[35]

To be *part of a crowd* is to be in untruth; for Kierkegaard, truth, as we have already seen, lies only in the individual's existence and his reflection on it. That his own concern with the task of awakening the awareness of existence in his audience by means of indirect communication is developed within the domain of Christianity is interesting and important; it is not essential.

[34] *CUP,* p. 216.
[35] *The Point of View,* p. 115.

What is essential is the energy—and historically speaking, the success—of Kierkegaard's development of his thesis that *the individual stands alone.*[36] For Kierkegaard there is no *settled* human nature. There is no truth or revelation which is not an occasion for reflection regarding its validity or source. There is not even a personal continuity which man can simply take for granted. But there is insight into the uniqueness of human subjectivity, the spiritual development of which is not an object of presumption but of self-activity.[37] There is also insight into the fact that such activity on the part of the self is not essentially rational, but involves co-ordinately reason, imagination, and feeling[38]—and not just as three separate factors:

> The task is not to exalt the one at the expense of the other, but to give them an equal status, to unify them in simultaneity; the medium in which they are unified is existence.[39]

[36] *CUP,* p. 287.
[37] *CUP,* p. 309.
[38] *CUP,* p. 310.
[39] *CUP,* p. 311.

Nietzsche: The Meaning of the Earth

2

Verily, the earth shall yet become a site of recovery. And even now a new fragrance surrounds it, bringing salvation—and a new hope.

FRIEDRICH NIETZSCHE, Thus Spoke Zarathustra

If Kierkegaard is the father of contemporary existentialism, Nietzsche is its tutor. Kierkegaard is a philosopher of existence; Nietzsche is a philosopher of *life* and of *the world.*

At the outset of this study I proposed two criteria by which to adjudge a philosopher an existentialist: namely, that he engage in an analysis of the nature of human existence, and that he pursue the task of making other men aware of their existence and its *essential* freedom. Nietzsche does not strongly exhibit either of these characteristics in his writings. Why then should an entire chapter in a study of existentialism be devoted to him?

The answer to this question rests upon an ambiguity in the use of the term "existentialism" in this study. If an existential philosophy is a philosophy exhibiting one or both of the two characteristics I have noted, the nineteenth and twentieth centuries are not the only two periods in which existential philosophies have appeared. This needs no more illustration than the teachings of Socrates as recorded in the dialogues of Plato. Existentialism, in other words, is a type of philosophizing of which the Socratic philosophy is one example and contemporary existentialism another. The significance of Nietzsche with respect to existentialism lies in the fact that in his work we find much of the *thematic material* whose incorporation into contemporary existentialism has given it much of its characteristic flavor. The discussions that follow state this thematic material and show its organic interrelatedness within Nietzsche's thinking, reserving to later chapters the task of illustrating the recurrence of these themes in the writings of contemporary existentialists.

Approaching Nietzsche in search of a coherent philosophy, one may easily question whether there is any interrelatedness in his thought, so great a turbulence is manifested in it. There is turbulence also in Kierkegaard's thinking, but in his case it is, as it were, self-imposed. As he himself puts it:

> . . . the development of the subject consists precisely in his active interpenetration of himself by reflection concerning his own existence, so that he really thinks what he thinks through making a reality of it.[1]

Unlike Kierkegaard, Nietzsche does not believe that reflection is an action in which we engage; rather, it is an action that engages us:

> A thought comes when "it" will and not when "I" will. It is thus a *falsification* of the evidence to say that the subject "I" conditions the predicate "think." [2]

Conscious thought, human prejudice notwithstanding, is for Nietzsche an activity dominated by instinct and the interrelation and interaction of our drives.[3] These instincts and drives are themselves aspects of the basic energy, the "intelligible character" of the universe, the Will to Power:

> . . . would you have a name for my world? A *solution* of all your riddles? Do you also want a light, you most concealed, strongest men . . . ? *This world is the Will to Power—and nothing else!* And even you yourselves are this will to power—and nothing besides! [4]

[1] Kierkegaard, *Concluding Unscientific Postscript,* p. 151.

[2] Friedrich Nietzsche, *Beyond Good and Evil* (Chicago: Henry Regnery Co., 1955), p. 18. This reference hereafter cited as *BGE.*

[3] *BGE,* p. 3; p. 42.

[4] Friedrich Nietzsche, *The Will to Power,* II, trans. Ludovici, Levy, ed. (London: George Allen & Unwin Ltd., 1924), p. 432. This reference hereafter cited as *WP.*

On his own grounds, it appears that the turbulence in Nietzsche's thinking is itself a reflection of the turbulence of a world behind which stands the Will to Power:

> And do you know what "the universe" is to my mind? . . . This universe is a monster of energy, without beginning or end . . . a sea of forces storming and raging in itself, for ever changing. . . .[5]

This powerful picture of the world conceived as energy in ceaseless ebb and flow is superimposed upon the metaphor of a cosmic will in Nietzsche's notion of the will to power. The metaphor of will as an ultimate reality underlying the particular objects and events of the universe seems to have been borrowed by Nietzsche from Arthur Schopenhauer, a German philosopher who had developed from the metaphor of will a comprehensive theory of life and the world.[6] Aside from the analogous role which the concept of will plays in the respective philosophies of these two men, we find that Nietzsche respects Schopenhauer's matter-of-fact acceptance of such an un-Christian view of the world. It is against the background of such a world-view that Schopenhauer, according to Nietzsche, has posed the question:

> *Has existence then a significance at all?*—the question which will require a couple of centuries even to be completely heard in all its profundity.[7]

Nietzsche himself does not wish existence to be divested of its ambiguous character.[8] Somewhat differently yet more forcefully he states that the secret to the greatest fruitfulness and enjoyment of existence is *to live dangerously*.[9] The worth of a life lived dangerously is underscored in *Thus Spoke Zarathustra* when the prophet Zarathustra volunteers to bury with his own hands a dying tightrope walker because the latter had lost his life in the pursuit of a vocation of danger.[10] In contrast to the scientific and philosophical pursuit

[5] *WP,* II, p. 431.

[6] See Arthur Schopenhauer, *The Philosophy of Schopenhauer,* ed. Edman (New York: Random House Inc., 1928).

[7] Friedrich Nietzsche, *Joyful Wisdom* (New York: Frederick Ungar Publishing Company, 1960), p. 309. This reference hereafter cited as *JW*.

[8] *JW,* p. 339.

[9] *JW,* p. 219.

[10] Friedrich Nietzsche, *Thus Spoke Zarathustra,* in *The Portable Nietzsche,* ed. Kaufmann (New York: The Viking Press, Inc., 1960), pp. 131-132. This reference hereafter cited as *TSZ*.

of a "world of truth," a debasement of existence, which renders it but "a ready-reckoner exercise and calculation for stay-at-home mathematicians,"[11] Nietzsche praises the life of ambiguity and danger.

Moreover, it is our earthly life that Nietzsche holds sacred. Unlike the Christian conception of existence in which life on earth is merely a path toward a future sacred existence, Nietzsche's conception holds that ". . . *existence is considered sacred enough* to justify even a tremendous amount of suffering."[12] This is the tragic view of existence: the proper view for man.

And, indeed, it is for ". . . man alone, of all the animals, that there are no *eternal* horizons or perspectives."[13] The traditional schema of the universe, the maps by which Western man has oriented his life, are beginning to dissolve and lose their force. Nietzsche sees in the nineteenth century an advent of nihilism, "the radical rejection of value, meaning, and desirability."[14] In rejecting the false interpretation of the world imposed by Christianity, the West has become suspicious of all interpretations of the world and has turned to nihilism.[15] It had been but a conceit on the part of Western man to think that the whirlpool of forces within which he stood was rational and possessed a rational aim.[16]

But for Nietzsche the absence of eternal horizons, the lack of a rational structure or purpose in the universe, is not in itself a justification for a nihilistic orientation—which is to say, no orientation at all:

> We require, at some time, new values.[17]

More explicitly, man requires new values not only in respect to shaping his life (although that is certainly a major concern of Nietzsche's), but also in respect to determining the significance of the world, the ambit within which that life is lived. From the point of view of an uncritical common sense, it seems unusual to speak of man's "determining the significance of the world." Presumably

[11] *JW,* pp. 338-339.
[12] Friedrich Nietzsche, "Notes 1888," in *The Portable Nietzsche,* p. 459.
[13] *JW,* p. 180.
[14] *WP,* I, p. 5. See also Kaufmann's translation in *Existentialism from Dostoevsky to Sartre,* p. 110.
[15] *WP,* I, p. 5.
[16] Nietzsche, "Notes 1875," in *The Portable Nietzsche,* p. 50.
[17] *WP,* I, Preface, p. 2. See also Kaufmann's translation.

either the world possesses significance or it does not. The matter would seem to be not under human jurisdiction in much the same way that, to most observers, the beauty of the rose lies in the rose, not in the eye of the viewer. This is not, however, the manner in which Nietzsche interprets the subject of significance, of value generally:

> It is we, who think and feel, that actually and unceasingly *make* something which did not before exist: the whole eternally increasing world of valuations, colors, weights, perspectives, gradations, affirmations and negations. . . . Whatever has *value* in the present world, has not it in itself, by its nature—nature is always worthless—but a value was once given to it, bestowed upon it and it was *we* who gave and bestowed! We only have created the world *which is of any account to man!* [18]

Nietzsche's acceptance of this human basis for the fact of the appearance of value in the world, and, for that matter, *the value of the world,* has important consequences for the direction of his philosophy, especially with respect to his oftenmentioned conception of the overman and the role which the overman is to fill. The point here, that man is *responsible* for attributing significance to the world, is remarkably similar to Kierkegaard's assertion that man is *responsible* for the use to which he puts *his life*. Nietzsche's intent is to commend to man a positive valuation of the world, but it is not sufficient simply to assert that this intent is opposed to the Christian devaluation of this world in favor of a life hereafter. Christianity is not, indeed, relevant and man *must* set his own values; for, after all, *God is dead.*

Nietzsche speaks of the death of God frequently in his writings, but nowhere more tellingly than in the beautiful episode in *Joyful Wisdom* in which a madman runs into the market-place, calling, "I seek God! I seek God!" His audience, composed in part of nonbelievers, is lightly amused until the madman captures their attention with his cry that God is gone because he and the spectators there in the market-place have killed Him. This murder of God is not without its cosmic consequences. Where does the earth move now? Where do we move if not in a directionless space, an "infinite nothingness" which now becomes colder and darker? Yet the murdering of God is an occasion for awe, certainly a deed of too great a magnitude for mere man to have accomplished it:

[18] *JW,* pp. 235-236.

> ". . . Shall we not ourselves have to become Gods, merely to seem worthy of it? There never was a greater event—and on account of it, all who are born after us belong to a higher history than any history hitherto!"[19]

At this point the madman becomes silent, for he realizes that he has come too soon; men have murdered God, but the news and the significance of the event have not yet reached their ears.[20]

This powerful passage depicts the decay, not of the institution of Christianity—for, perhaps symbolically, the madman does leave the market-place and enters various churches to recite a requiem—but of the orientation in values and morals which has traditionally been derived from Christianity. With God dead, there is no longer up or down, no longer a metaphysical prop for the directedness of our lives.

But only a negative connotation should not be attributed to Nietzsche's metaphor of the death of God. On the contrary, the lack of a divine order implies no lack of value, for the horizon, even if not bright, is at least open once again:

> . . . our ships can at last put out to sea in face of every danger; every hazard is again permitted to the discerner; the sea, *our* sea, again lies open before us; perhaps never before did such an "open sea" exist. . . .[21]

Furthermore, the open horizon is a horizon of *this* world, not of some "true" realm beyond appearance or beyond the clouds. If this world is the "apparent" world, still it is not merely apparent; its reality is in no way dependent on a "true" world which would be conceived as serving as a transcendent ground or *raison d'être.*

> . . . the "true" world is merely added by a lie.[22]

Nietzsche's polemics against the notion of a world lying beyond experience yet somehow envisioned as being more basic in the nature of things are two-edged; they aim at both the Christian and the philosophical postulations of "other" worlds—especially, in the latter case, at those of Immanuel Kant. Both theological and meta-

[19] *JW,* p. 168.
[20] *JW,* pp. 167-169.
[21] *JW,* p. 276.
[22] Friedrich Nietzsche, *Twilight of the Idols,* in *The Portable Nietzsche,* p. 481. This reference hereafter cited as *TO.*

physical conceptions of another world appear in the thinking of Kant. Faced with the question "why be moral," Kant's ultimate answer, his often nobler intentions notwithstanding, is anchored in the hope that there will be a never-ending life after death, a life during which God, the object of another hope—entitled "postulate" by Kant—will reward us for our earthly virtue. (One might call this bit of Kantian ethics the "Lollipop Theory" of morality.) Thus for Kant, whom Nietzsche dubs the "underhanded Christian," the center of gravity for this life is removed from earthly existence and is transferred to a life after death, where it appears in the guise of the awkwardly earthly notion of a reward.

On the other hand, and in a metaphysical vein, the philosophy of Kant includes a conception of a realm of *things in themselves;* that is, of a realm of entities whose action upon our organs of sense causes us to "have" experience. On this view, the world which we encounter *in* our experience is a construction, a private possession of each person having experience, rather than the commonly possessed, publicly observable world that it seems to be. Both this technical conception of another realm of existence and the theological conception of an after-life or heaven are, according to Nietzsche, genuinely conceptions of *what is not.* To claim a knowledge of such transcendent realms is to spin fables. The very belief that such realms are set over against *this* world is only a suggestion of decadence, a symptom of the *decline of life.*[23] But no such decadent view, no "sneaky ruses" lie before the healthy body of which Zarathustra says:

> . . . it speaks of the meaning of the earth.[24]

Although the advent of the overman is an explicit corollary of the death of God, the reinstatement of the significance of the earth is nevertheless of equal, if not greater, importance to Nietzsche. With the death of God, ". . . nobody is held responsible any longer . . ." for the world:

> . . . that alone is the great liberation; with this alone is the innocence of becoming restored. The concept of "God" was until now the greatest objection to existence. We deny God, we deny the responsibility in God: *only thereby do we redeem the world.*[25]

[23] *TO,* p. 484.
[24] *TSZ,* p. 145.
[25] *TO,* p. 501. Italics mine.

Man, not God, redeems the world by becoming himself the creator of the world;[26] and the world thus redeemed, its new value achieved, will be a site of recovery, and a place for the overman.[27]

Who then is this Nietzschean overman? Because of the emphasis on the overman in Nietzsche's philosophy as well as out of respect to the lively and often scholarly debates regarding the precise meaning to be given to this notion, I must digress for a moment from the exposition of Nietzsche's thought to sketch the background for my own interpretation of the overman concept. As previously noted, I do not consider Nietzsche a "full member" of the existentialist camp, if only because of his generally negative attitudes toward the existentialistic concern with the fact of consciousness and with free will.[28] Nevertheless, many of his themes have been woven into contemporary existentialism, especially in the case of Sartre. In the few pages that follow, therefore, the reader will find neither the biological superman of the Nazis nor the half "saint," half "genius" of Nietzsche himself.[29]

On the contrary, the conception of the overman that I propose here is based on a question put by the madman after his proclamation of the death of God. Although already quoted before, it is worth repeating; speaking of the murder of God, the madman says:

> . . . Shall we not ourselves have to become Gods, merely to seem worthy of it? [30]

Although the death of God in this passage is clearly a metaphor, it seems to describe, albeit in figurative language, an actual experience of Western man. Differently put: the metaphor of the death of God seems to point out an experience which many persons have had, an experience of the world, not a world in which God is nonexistent, but a world from which God has departed. There is a difference between experiencing the truth of atheism and the truth of the death of God. In the first case, one need merely report that

[26] *TSZ,* p. 198.
[27] *TSZ,* p. 189.
[28] Cf., e.g., *BGE,* pp. 17-25.
[29] See Walter Kaufmann, *Nietzsche* (New York: Meridian Books, The World Publishing Company, Inc., 1956), p. 271, for emphasis on this conception of the overman.
[30] *JW,* p. 168.

among the "furniture of the universe" is not included—and never was included, for that matter—the being of God. In the second case, the report is that among the many items that populate the universe there are many whose validity, force, and significance depended on the existence of God and on the orientation of our existence toward the divine scheme of things; and God is *no longer* included in the scheme.

Consider, for example, an atheist or agnostic who has long viewed morality as an expedient generally agreed to and followed by members of society. Contrast this atheist or agnostic with a young believer, reared as a Christian or Jew, who, during his college career, for example, simultaneously experiences both the disintegration of his childhood faith and a downward trend, a lowering of standards, in his personal life. It must be granted that the individual who regards morals as merely expedient could not experience a poignant personal problem similar to that suffered by our hypothetical college student. But in the case of the individual whose faith is weakening and who is faced with the need to make painful personal decisions, there is a peculiar dimension to the situation, a dimension which would not exist in the case of the atheist or agnostic. Perhaps the dimension can be metaphorically characterized as the intersection of the *now present* positive aspects of the problem at hand with the *formerly present but now conspicuously absent* source of authority or instruction. There is an understanding of the relevant value as well as of the "proper" implementation, but there is an absence of that being, God, who alone can judge the validity of the relevant values and enjoin that they be followed in solving the problem-ridden situation. The painfulness of decision is increased by the conjunction of two different levels of awareness, awareness of relevant values, but also awareness of a lack of ground for those values. This experience, analogous to what will later be termed "abandonment" by Sartre, is the negative aspect of the death of God.

On the positive side—and bringing us closer to interpreting the meaning of the overman—unless God is dead, human freedom is not complete. There is, as Dostoyevsky so beautifully portrayed in *The Brothers Karamazov,* a freedom to choose between good and evil. But there is not a freedom to go *beyond good and evil.* This freedom can be achieved only upon the occasion of the death of God, the annihilation of the constricting force of all schemes of values, especially the Christian ones. Zarathustra is "the destroyer of morality." [31]

Nietzsche's overman is the person who has become god-like by murdering God; that is, he is the person who not only chooses between good and evil, but who himself *establishes new values and affirms the significance of life in so doing,* just as the God of the Old Testament established commandments. But whereas, according to Nietzsche, the commandments of God constituted a denial of life,[32] those of the overman are an affirmation of life. The essential point is that the value of life is not legislated from on high, but is affirmed by the overman within a context pre-eminently dangerous, a context in which neither in fact nor in belief are there any metaphysical supports or justifications for such an affirmation.

The overman is one who seeks to become, *to achieve,* what he is to be—

> . . . the new, the unique, the incomparable, making laws for ourselves and creating ourselves.[33]

Philosophers are to fill this need for a re-emphasis of self-creation and self-legislation regarding values; they are to be spirits strong and original, men who will teach that "man's future is man's *will,* dependent on man's will." [34] They will be, not spectators of the universe as past philosophers have often been, but *commanders* and *legislators:*

> They say, "It *shall* be thus!" They determine the "whither" and the "to what end" of mankind—having the preliminary work of all the workers in philosophy, the overpowerers of the past, at their disposal. But they grope with creative hands toward the future. . . . Their "knowing" is *creating*. Their creating is legislative.[35]

Their freedom is not only a Kierkegaardian will to assume responsibility for themselves,[36] but also and especially a freedom to ". . .

[31] Friedrich Nietzsche, *Ecco Homo,* in *The Philosophy of Nietzsche,* trans. Clifton Fadiman (New York: Random House, Inc., 1937), p. 53. This reference hereafter cited as *EH.*

[32] Friedrich Nietzsche, *The Antichrist,* in *The Portable Nietzsche,* pp. 594-595.

[33] *JW,* p. 263.

[34] *BGE,* pp. 114-115.

[35] *BGE,* p. 135.

[36] *TO,* p. 542.

bid farewell to every belief, to every wish for certainty. . . ." [37] These philosophers, the overmen—and I see no reason to believe that Nietzsche conceived of the overman as something to be achieved only by *the few*—are men gladdened by the death of God. It is they for whom the horizons are open once more in that they see the *infinity* of the world, not the astronomer's infinity of space and time, but the adventurer's infinity of ambiguity, of openness to interpretation.[38]

They are men who say Yes to life even in the face of the strangest and hardest problems,[39] while, at the same time, viewing death as a consummation to life, as "a spur and promise to the survivors," [40] *the living.*

Death for Nietzsche is not a mere happening that befalls an individual, but a free act not different in kind from other acts one might choose to do, "the holy No when the time for Yes has passed." [41] There is question whether suicide constitutes here a meaningful alternative for Nietzsche; to die fighting certainly does.[42] However death comes about, Nietzsche's point seems to be that death should be illuminated by a *meaning* issuing from within the life which is ending:

> That your dying be no blasphemy against man and earth, my friends, that I ask of the honey of your soul. . . .
>
> Thus I want to die myself that you, my friends, may love the earth more for my sake. . . .[43]

Kierkegaard rediscovered the *individual.* Nietzsche gave him a new *earth* to walk upon.

[37] *JW,* p. 287.
[38] *JW,* p. 341.
[39] *TO,* p. 562.
[40] *TSZ,* p. 183.
[41] *TSZ,* p. 185.
[42] *TSZ,* p. 184.
[43] *TSZ,* pp. 185-186.

Husserl: The Transcendental Turn

3

That we should set aside all previous habits of thought, see through and break down the mental barriers which these habits have set along the horizons of our thinking, and in full intellectual freedom proceed to lay hold on those genuine philosophical problems still awaiting completely fresh formulation which the liberated horizons on all sides disclose to us—these are hard demands. Yet nothing less is required.

EDMUND HUSSERL, Ideas

A feature common to the philosophical thought of both Kierkegaard and Nietzsche is a certain mistrust of the erection of comprehensive philosophical systems within which all aspects of reality, including human existence, find well-defined niches. Kierkegaard, for example, writes:

> So-called pantheistic systems have often been characterized and challenged in the assertion that they abrogate the distinction between good and evil, and destroy freedom. . . . Every system must be pantheistic precisely on account of its finality. Existence must be revoked in the external before the system can round itself out; there must be no existing remainder, not even such a little minikin as the existing Herr Professor who writes the system.[1]

[1] Kierkegaard, *Concluding Unscientific Postscript,* p. 111.

Lacking Kierkegaard's humor but exhibiting the same disregard for system is Nietzsche's:

> I mistrust all systematizers and I avoid them. The will to a system is a lack of integrity.[2]

In Kierkegaard the repudiation of system-building assumes positive form in a monumental concern for the reflective and decisive human being. Nietzsche scorns system-building in an unashamedly pagan exaltation of the meaning of the earth and of an existence oriented to the earth. It is likely that, had they lived in the twentieth century, both Kierkegaard and Nietzsche, the passionately involved precursors of modern existentialism, would have looked upon the works of Edmund Husserl, German logician and philosopher, with a jaundiced eye.

Husserl's major published works show no great concern with freedom or decisiveness, with danger or fidelity to the earth.[3] There is evidence, however, of all those qualities which would have led to his being quickly labeled—and condemned—as a system-builder: comprehensiveness of scheme, certainty regarding both the absoluteness of his method and of his conclusions, disregard of the contingencies evinced in the unfolding of events and of the risks involved in existence—all these set forth in an often obscure, ponderous terminology. Could such a figure, whatever judgment be made of his genius, have any but a negative relevance to the philosophy of existence? I propose to develop two affirmative answers to this question by showing first that Husserl's method of philosophizing, entitled *phenomenology,* provides an approach by means of which it becomes possible to overcome *some* of the phenomenalistic tendencies introduced into modern philosophy by the influence of René Descartes. There is a sense, to be explicated in the discussions that follow, in which Husserl not only fails to transcend Cartesian subjectivism, but even strengthens it. However, other aspects of Husserl's approach prepare the way for a metaphysical reinstatement of the *immediate* reality of the world, a reinstatement that dovetails in a singularly harmonious manner with Nietzsche's re-emphasis of

[2] Nietzsche, *The Twilight of the Idols,* in *The Portable Nietzsche,* p. 470.

[3] An exception is Husserl's last publication, *The Crisis of the European Sciences and Transcendental Phenomenology*. See Herbert Spiegelberg, "Husserl's Phenomenology and Existentialism," *The Journal of Philosophy,* LVII, No. 2 (January 21, 1960), p. 66, footnote.

the world. The axiological contribution of Nietzsche and the metaphysical contribution of Husserl make available much of the material needed for the detailed analyses of existence *in the world* provided by Heidegger, Sartre, and other existentialists.

Secondly, I propose to show that Husserl, while pursuing his primary aim of clarifying the methods of phenomenology, incidentally develops a metaphysics of the relation between the self and the world. Although this metaphysics is not adopted as such by the existentialists who follow him, it is influential in shaping the methods and concepts of these later thinkers. More importantly, the self-world metaphysics developed by Husserl becomes, in the existentialism of the twentieth century, a convenient *form* into which a *matter* largely derived from the philosophies of Kierkegaard and Nietzsche can be cast. Perhaps too generally but not misleadingly stated: contemporary existentialism is in most of its essential characteristics the product of the application of a methodology based on Husserl's phenomenology to thematic material introduced into Western thinking (and feeling) by the reflections of Kierkegaard and Nietzsche.

In order to develop the first point regarding Husserl's relation to existentialism, it is necessary to review briefly some phases of Descartes' thinking on the relation between the self and the world and thus clarify the phenomenalistic influence which Descartes' philosophy has had. We shall then look at Husserl's main criticism of Descartes and see how Husserl avoids the Cartesian subjectivism. In the pursuit of these objectives, the meaning of Husserl's phenomenology will be clarified.

René Descartes, a seventeenth-century French philosopher, is generally accorded the title of father of modern philosophy, primarily because of the way in which he shifted the emphasis of Western philosophy from a concern with the world in itself to a concern with the possibility of *our knowledge* of the world. Although philosophers had always dealt with the problem of the nature of knowledge, Descartes' predecessors had for the most part handled this problem within a context in which the *existence* of the world was presupposed and only the mode and extent of our knowledge of it were considered problematic. Since the dissemination of the ideas of Descartes, contained in *Meditations on the First Philosophy* (that is, metaphysics), the existence of the world is no longer the object of a presupposition but, at best, the conclusion of a debate and, at worst, a fact forever beyond human ken.

The arguments by which Descartes rendered questionable the existence of the physical world are developed in a series of meditations upon the nature and possibility of our knowledge of God and the world. Descartes' *Meditations* stem from his concern over the fact that from his youth on he has accepted as true many opinions which he now knows to be false. In view of this past acceptance and with a desire to rid himself of all false opinions in order to reconstruct his knowledge on an indubitable foundation, Descartes addresses himself to the question: On what grounds can I undermine *all* of my present opinions, not one by one, but rather all at one fell swoop, *on grounds of principle?* Since Descartes' opinions, according to his analysis, are based either on sense experience or on reasoning, only these two modes of obtaining knowledge have to be examined with respect to their reliability as grounds for positively true belief.

Descartes' conclusions, with which one can scarcely disagree (at least, not without changing, as Husserl does, the nature of the problem itself), are negative. For, on the one hand, we have all at some time or other been deceived by the senses; illusions, if not commonplace, are possible and are occasionally experienced. It is also the case, with respect to all sense awareness, that there are no incontestable means of distinguishing dreams from waking life.[4] Shakespeare may well have stated a philosophical truth in *The Tempest*:

> We are such stuff
> As dreams are made on, and our little life
> Is rounded with a sleep.

With respect to reasoning, on the other hand, Descartes sees that by the same token that he has on occasion judged others to be wrong on matters of which they felt certain, he must admit that he himself may be deceived in making judgments and calculations.[5]

If both the contents of awareness and the processes of thought can be called in question on grounds of principle, what then is left that cannot be doubted? The fact that Descartes, a doubter, exists. However questionable may be all of one's beliefs, however accidental the relations of beliefs to the mind of the believer, the existence of the mind of the believer—when he doubts or believes—is itself

[4] René Descartes, "Meditations," *A Discourse on Method and Selected Writings*, trans. Veitch (New York: E. P. Dutton & Co., 1951), pp. 87-88. This reference hereafter cited as *Med.*

[5] Descartes, *Med.*, p. 90.

beyond question. Of this Descartes is certain: his existence as *a thinking thing.*[6]

A predisposition to an existentialistic point of view is not necessary in order to ask: But what about the *world?* Part of Descartes' answer to this question serves to illustrate what I have termed the phenomenalistic influence of his thinking. It has already been stated that the one absolutely certain fact for Descartes, the only belief which he cannot in principle doubt, is the fact that he, Descartes, insofar as he is doubting, necessarily exists. Not the man, the complete psycho-physical organism, but only the mind, "a thinking thing," [7] is known to exist with this certainty. (For example, the mind might only be dreaming that it is somehow attached to a body.) Elsewhere Descartes states this point in the following manner:

> . . . I thence concluded that I was a substance whose whole essence or nature consists only in thinking, and which, that it may exist, has need of no place, nor is dependent on any material thing; so that "I," that is to say, the mind by which I am what I am, is wholly distinct from the body. . . .[8]

The notion of substance is employed here by Descartes to denote that the mind, the "I," is a substratum, an underlying ground, for the various "thoughts" which the mind has. Differently stated, doubts, understanding, affirmation, denial, volition, refusal, imagination, and perception (all of which are comprehended by the term "thought")[9] are all *accidents* of the *substance* which is the mind, in a manner analogous to the way that hardness, brownness, and rectangularity are accidents of the substance that is the table top on which I now write. Various accidents come and go, but the underlying substance remains the same; the substance is the independently real foundation for the accidents, themselves unable to exist in isolation from their substantial base.

Descartes' thesis regarding the perceived world—which world, following Nietzsche, is the one that here concerns us, the *apparent* world being the *real* world—is that all that we *really* have is *our*

[6] Descartes, *Med.*, p. 96.

[7] Descartes, *Med.*, p. 96.

[8] René Descartes, *A Discourse on Method,* p. 28. This reference hereafter cited as *Dis.*

[9] Descartes, *Med.*, p. 98.

perceptions just insofar as they are perceptions. We can view these perceptions two different ways, to be sure, but neither manner of viewing changes the situation regarding the status of the *perceived world* essentially. Our ideas or perceptions may be taken as only modes of consciousness (which is to say, merely as accidents inhering in the substance that is the mind), in which case there is no difference among them; they are just different items present to awareness. Or we may take perceptions as images representing substances; as such they differ among themselves to the extent that some of the substances represented have a greater or a lesser degree of reality in themselves—for example, God and stones. However, the fact remains that these perceptions are still just perceptions, although they are now being considered in their capacity of signifying real objects.[10] *The real world remains outside our awareness;* our ideas and perceptions are only links connecting our awareness with the world. Strictly speaking, for Descartes we are not aware of the world. And since, as stated in the passage quoted above, the mind "has need of no place," *it cannot really be said that we are in the world.* Husserl and, later, the existentialists have a very brief reply to Descartes: *we are in the world.* Where then did Descartes' thinking go astray?

The significance of this question is underscored by the fact that Husserl greatly respects Descartes' contributions to philosophy, especially the method of doubt, briefly outlined above, as it occurs in Descartes' *Meditations.* Not only did Descartes, according to Husserl, *turn to the subject,* in that for Descartes, as well as for Husserl, the philosopher should make no appeals to knowledge or principles which the philosopher *as an individual* cannot underwrite; but Descartes also turns to the subject in that the method of doubt provides a means by which the subject, the Ego, and his thoughts are given their deserved centrality in the philosophical enterprise.[11]

Where Descartes made his crucial mistake is, as Husserl views the matter, in failing to make *the transcendental turn.* That is, Descartes, instead of proceeding to make an analysis only of the Ego and its thoughts and perceptions, fell back on the traditions of medieval philosophy and illegitimately imported into his thinking certain principles that cannot be verified simply by the analysis of

[10] Descartes, *Med.,* p. 110.

[11] Edmund Husserl, *Cartesian Meditations,* trans. Cairns (The Hague: N. V. Martinus Nijhoff's, 1960), pp. 2-3. This reference hereafter cited as *C. Med.*

the Ego and its experiences. For example, in order to justify the validity of most of our experiences of the world, Descartes had to make use of his belief in the goodness of God, a God who would certainly not have created us in such a manner that our experiences would be generally deceptive.[12] For Descartes, our experiences are known to be relevant to the world because God in his goodness guarantees this relevance; the phenomenal nature of these experiences is transcended only indirectly by the appeal to a principle which is not open to inspection *within experience*, the principle of the nondeceitful nature of God.

Husserl's transcendental turn avoids the importation of such principles, which from the phenomenological point of view are considered prejudices. By implication then, the transcendental turn involves seeing that *our experiences are directly of the world*, that there is not a *dichotomy* but only a *polarity* between a self having experiences and a world underlying that experience. The purpose of phenomenology is in part to help philosophers overcome the habit of thinking in terms of such vicious dichotomies and *to look at things in a new way*.

I have just mentioned phenomenology and the phenomenological point of view. In order to look further into Husserl's specific contributions, we must clarify what the phenomenological viewpoint means and what a phenomenologist sets out to accomplish. Usually a philosopher writes in order to convince the reader of the truth of what he has to say, that the world is as the writer has argued that it must be. The assertions of a philosopher, in other words, are intended to be true, although they may in fact be false, or perhaps even meaningless. Now to a certain extent, this objective also applies to the writings of phenomenologists. There is, however, an important difference between an essay in phenomenology and one in another type of philosophy: namely, whereas a philosopher in a field other than phenomenology writes in order to express certain facts about the world, a phenomenologist, as noted, writes in part in order to bring about on the part of the reader a certain *manner of viewing one's experience* (awareness) *of the world*.

One might say that all philosophers really intend that their works should have some such effect, but to raise this point as an objection to the uniqueness of phenomenology by thus down-

[12] Descartes, *Dis.*, pp. 33-34.

grading the role that viewing plays in it would be to obscure the contribution that phenomenology offers. Another response to this possible objection would be to point out that, whether Berkeley be right in saying that the world is composed of ideas or Democritus in saying that it is composed of matter, the world which is accessible to our experience *remains qualitatively the same.* Indeed, this qualitative sameness of the world in the face of—and in spite of—the disputes of metaphysicians is perhaps the main fact on which positivists have based their many attacks on traditional metaphysics. A third reply to this hypothetical objection takes the form of actually illustrating the manner in which phenomenologists do view the world.

What now follows is an attempt to lead the reader to a position from which he may view the world from one of the standpoints developed by phenomenology. It is difficult to achieve such a standpoint, especially since merely accepting as true what the phenomenologist asserts is by no means a guarantee that one will succeed in viewing the world as the phenomenologist views it. In this case, as in the case regarding subjectivity discussed in Chapter 1, all arguments and illustrations used are but means to an end, but ultimately it is the reader who will or will not successfully employ the means and thus gain the end in question.

The first step in attempting to gain one of the standpoints of phenomenology is to review briefly the nature of the world as conceived by common sense, as accessible to everyday experience. Some of the features of this world, and here I make no attempt to be comprehensive or over-systematic, are the following: the world is for the most part composed of physical objects spread out in both space and time and exhibiting a regularity of behavior that is often predictable by law; the world is inhabited by people that differ from mere objects in that the reality of a person is not exhausted by his physical make-up and is enhanced and, in a sense, crowned by the having of a self (a self which may be "ornery" or strange, but is essentially the same as our selves); the objects in the world have the qualities of being beautiful or ugly, useful or troublesome, natural or artificial; the people are good or evil, interesting or dull, energetic or slothful. Finally, it must be noted that most of the objects and persons in the world are real; only some have the quality of having been presented in illusion, delusion, or dream. These, then, constitute some of the *givens,* the data, of the world.

The transition from this everyday world to a standpoint in

phenomenology, if it is to be successfully made, may perhaps be facilitated by following two suggestions:

First, reconsider the list given above of features of the world, and note that none of the items in the list are such that any person of normal intelligence and outlook could possibly doubt them.

Second, ask yourself in what manner the features included in the list *are given* to one's awareness, for example:

a) In what manner is a physical object given? Is it not the case that, unless mirrors be used, we see only one side at a time? Do we ever see the inside of a physical object without rupturing it, let alone see *all* of it?
b) In what way is regularity of behavior given, especially since we simply do not keep many of the objects believed to behave regularly under any observation other than that of a purely accidental or casual variety?
c) In what way is another self given? Or is only the body "inhabited" by a self given? If so, how do we answer the questions raised in (a) above; that is, how is the "inhabitant" of a body given?
d) In what way is the usefulness of an object, or the slothfulness of a person, given?
e) Finally, in what way are *a world* and *one's being in that world* given?

From the standpoint of common sense, these questions do not arise, nor, for that matter, would anyone have reason to list features of the world as I have done here. In point of fact, anyone who would raise such questions within any "normal" context of discourse would probably not meet with a very sympathetic reception. The reason for such an unsympathetic reaction is simple: all of the items that are here being submitted to examination are so undeniably a part of what one means by "the world" that to question their nature or validity is to give evidence that one does not really *understand the world;* in short, that one is mentally deranged.

There is a sense in which the phenomenologist does not "understand" the world; there is also a sense in which he does. The contrast between these two points of view should serve to complete this introduction to the role of *viewing* in phenomenology. The sense in which a phenomenologist understands the world is the sense in which we all do; the point is simply that we never have to clarify exactly what this sense is, since we are not ordinarily challenged regarding it. If challenged, our answer, and the phenomenologist's answer, could take the form of the list presented above of the features of the world.

The sense in which the phenomenologist does *not* understand the world is the sense illustrated by the set of questions suggested above. The phenomenologist shares *with us* the world and its indicated features; what we do not (ordinarily) share with him is his curiosity regarding the nature of the world and its features, not as they unquestioningly are for common sense, but as they *are given* to the awareness of the phenomenological observer. Common sense is not doubted by the phenomenologist; phenomenology is not skepticism and it certainly is not phenomenalism. Common sense is simply *held in suspense* in phenomenology; what is usually admitted into the real world with full-blown status is now asked to present its credentials. Human experience of the world, to state the matter from a radically different angle, is no longer treated as a means for analyzing the contents and laws of the world, but is now *itself* an object for analysis. *That we experience the world,* one might say, is the point of departure for common sense; that *there is experience having those characteristics that lead us to believe there is a world* is a point of departure for phenomenology. And *that there is someone having the experience of being in that world* is a problem providing the common ground between phenomenology and phenomenological existentialism, a point to be taken up for discussion later in this chapter, when Husserl's relation to existentialism will be delineated.

Before directing our attention to further selected aspects of Husserl's phenomenology, there is one more task at hand, illustration of the phenomenological standpoint by characterizing the standpoint of common sense (termed by Husserl "the thesis of the natural attitude") on our relation to the world. For common sense, the world as it *is* is the sum total of reality; my present relation to it can be defined in part by use of the ideas of containment and employment. I am contained in a room in an apartment in a city in a state . . . and so on until we arrive at the outermost container, the world. I am also employing a physical object (a pen) in order to be employed (as a writer and philosopher) by a university which is employed (as perpetuator of an intellectual tradition) . . . and so on until we arrive at an employment executed for its own sake. In such a manner can my natural attitude toward the world be characterized.

In achieving a phenomenological standpoint, in executing what is termed *the phenomenological reduction,* I withhold judgment concerning this world and my employment in it. My emphasis shifts to the problem of determining *how* such a world and my employment in it are given to my awareness. Restricting myself for the moment to the first of these problems, the world as given to awareness, my characterization of it within the phenomenological standpoint must be such that in it I do not presume the reality of the world of common sense, but only the reality of what is given to awareness *exactly as it is given.* For example, within the phenomenological standpoint I cannot presume the physical reality of the pen with which I now write. On the contrary, the pen itself is not given to my awareness, but only certain ordered sense impressions, visual, tactual, and auditory. I *see* certain colors of changing value, I *feel* a certain substantiality intimately related to the changing configuration of color, and I *hear* disconnected and irregular sounds; within the natural attitude, I would simply have said that I see and feel my pen and hear the sound which it makes on the paper.

Again within the phenomenological attitude, I do not presume that I am physically within the world; rather, I am aware of the set of ordered perceptions that are *of* my pen yet are not, as noted, the pen itself. As I direct my gaze toward these perceptions, I am also less acutely aware of other ordered perceptions that constitute a *background* for the perceptions of my pen. I may, of course, direct my gaze to some of these perceptions, thereby bringing them into focus and letting the perceptions of my pen fall into the somewhat shadowy background. In fact, this is a transcription of what usually occurs as I direct my attention to a thought which I wish to clarify to myself. (It must be noted that the thought to which my attention is directed is not to be identified with the subvocal speech by means of which I verbalize the thought any more than the pen itself is to be identified with any of the perceptions that I have of it.) Finally, beyond the vague but presented background there is, implicit in my perception although in no way "contained" materially within it, a fringe of "indeterminate reality" which is my perception of the world as the ground of my present experiences of the pen.[13] This implicit background of my ex-

[13] Edmund Husserl, *Ideas* (London: George Allen & Unwin, Ltd., 1952), p. 102. Excerpts are quoted with the permission of The Macmillan Company, New York.

perience is an ultimate experiential horizon always present insofar as my experiences are "of the world."

Having made the distinction between my *natural attitude* toward the world of common sense and the phenomenological standpoint which can be achieved by suspending judgment concerning the reality of that world and directing my view to the fact of its givenness, I can now attend to the problem of defining the nature of the "I" that suspends the natural attitude. My first characterization of the "I" is negative; the "I" is not my physical person. That this is so is implicit in the fact of my having suspended the natural attitude. My physical person, in short, is included in the class of those physical objects whose reality I can no longer presuppose, having suspended the natural attitude. And with the theoretical loss of the availability of my physical person as a means of defining the "I" there is also the loss of the "human Ego" in the sense of the historical person in the world in virtue of its *having* a body with which it is intimately *connected* and by means of which it is related to the world inhabited by the body.[14] The identification of the "I" with the "human Ego" fails for the same reason that the identification of the "I" with the physical person did; the definition of the "human Ego" as well as of the physical person requires as a necessary presupposition the reality of the world as in the natural attitude, but that reality is not available within the phenomenological standpoint.

What then is available, if anything, for the task of specifying the "I" even after the suspension of judgments of reality required by the transition to the phenomenological standpoint? Before answering this question, let us further complicate the situation with added theoretical considerations. Let us assume that the experiences of the phenomenological observer are lacking in that organization which, as an ingredient in most of our ordinary experiences, is responsible for our belief that what, in one sense, are merely *our experiences,* are, in another sense, experiences *of* a world. Even if such experiential disorganization were to obtain, the stream of our experience would still exist, as Husserl says, as

> . . . a *self-contained system of Being,* as a system of *Absolute Being,* into which nothing can penetrate, and from which nothing can escape; which has no spatio-temporal exterior, and can be inside no spatio-temporal system; which cannot experience causality from anything nor

[14] *Ideas,* p. 153.

> exert causality upon anything, it being presupposed that causality bears the normal sense of natural causality as a relation of dependence between realities.[15]

The "I" within the phenomenological standpoint is pure consciousness, a "transcendental Ego" to whom experiences are present and from whom radiate such acts as the "turning of one's attention to," reference to which was made above. It must be strongly emphasized with respect to the "transcendental Ego" that, although it can direct its glance in different ways and to different portions of the stream of experience, it itself is never given as part of the stream of experience. Rather, it is self-identical with respect to its own stream of experience, and is numerically different from other "transcendental Egos," each "living in" its own stream of experience.[16]

However, it must be emphasized that this transcendental Ego is still describable (under ordinary circumstances; not under conditions in which the usual organization of experience breaks down) as having experience *immediately of a world,* in contrast to the Cartesian conception of the mind whose experiences are private possessions on the basis of which it is inferred that there is a world. This same point can be illustrated by another consideration: if a Husserlian transcendental Ego suspends the phenomenological standpoint, that is, executes the phenomenological reduction, it then views itself as a human self (empirical Ego) spatially *in* the world of the natural attitude, that is, of common sense. But if a Cartesian mind suspends belief in the principles by which it infers the existence of the real world, it is left as a mind aware of perceptions which are *mere* perceptions rather than aspects of the world.

Before going on to illustrate further aspects of Husserl's phenomenology, I wish to emphasize the thesis originally proposed at the beginning of this chapter; namely, that the relevance of phenomenology to existentialism lies in just this Nietzschean insistence that the world of which we have direct experience is the real *and only* world, not just an organized set of experiences as suggested by Descartes. However, and this is an important qualification, the fact that our experiences are usually of the world is no

[15] *Ideas,* p. 153.

[16] *Ideas,* p. 172. Husserl later says that the pure Ego is given "together with" consciousness (*Ideas,* p. 173), a shift which, as we shall see, Sartre was quick to pounce upon.

guarantee for the continuing existence *or* nature of the world as perceived. The transcendental Ego is an absolute realm of being; the world *is not*. But, for better or for worse, it's the only world we have!

Although the discussions that have been presented up to this point have certainly not been without theoretical content, the central purpose in presenting them as I have has been to underscore as much as possible the extent to which the phenomenological enterprise rests on achieving a certain *point of view*. What follows is a statement of certain selected theses of phenomenology, theses which, according to Husserl, are discoverable by suspending the natural attitude toward the world and thereby achieving the phenomenological standpoint within which the appropriate investigations can then be made.

The type of investigation conducted by a phenomenologist can be characterized by seizing upon the very word "discoverable" used above, and recalling the now rare meaning of the word "discover." That meaning is to *disclose* or to *reveal* in the sense that something *is*, and in "discovering" it, we simply *un*-cover it, reveal it, open it to view. The object of a phenomenological investigation is, accordingly, to discover evidence, evidence being:

> . . . the *self-appearance*, the *self-exhibiting*, the *self-giving*, of an affair, an affair-complex (or state of affairs), a universality, a value, or other objectivity, in the final mode: "itself there." . . .[17]

Although it seems simple enough to understand that evidence for the phenomenologist is what is *itself there* in awareness, what is present to awareness, it is possible to miss some of the meaning of this concept of evidence unless it be contrasted with an example of nonevidence. To illustrate the difference: within the natural attitude, I know that I am now writing in a third floor apartment overlooking a street and some freshly mown lawns. However, it is evening now, and I cannot see the area clearly from where I sit. If I now suspend the natural attitude and ask *how* what I know about my location is given to me, the answer will be quite dissimilar to the description I sketched above. The street and lawns are not given in *evidence*, for I do not now have experience of them, but only of a darkness filling in my experience of the window frame. That I have had experiences of the street and lawns is true, but these ex-

[17] *C. Med.*, p. 57.

periences, being in the past, are not themselves *evidence* now, and my reference to them to justify the fact that *I know* the street and lawns are still there involves a presumption on my part. Note carefully that *my belief in the continuing existence of the street and lawns* is now given to me in evidence, but this is a belief and not the existence of the objects themselves.

The significance of the phenomenological concept of evidence can be further underscored, now that it has been illustrated, by exhibiting how it relates to the status of *theory* (in the sense of verified explanatory hypotheses as, for example, in the empirical sciences). Any happening of everyday concern to us is one that we feel we either "understand" or could in principle "understand" by means of a theory that "explains" the happening in question. An automobile motor that will not start in subzero weather, a headache, a neurosis, an eclipse—all of these events can be "understood" by means of some theory or other; that is to say, there are theories purporting to show how any one of these events is the resultant of a certain set of conditions, the conditions and the respective resultant having been found usually to occur together and in the appropriate sequence. Thus, confronted with a headache, many of us might say: "I've simply been worrying too much lately." The point here is that theories play a by no means small role in the organization and interpretation which we impose on our experiences.

This role of theory does not obtain, however, within the phenomenological standpoint, and for this reason: a theory is a mental construction based on evidence presented to us within the *natural attitude*. It follows, therefore, that a theory, being grounded as it is on the common-sense point of view which constitutes the natural attitude, presupposes the existence of the world and a degree of regularity of behavior on the part of the objects making up the world. However, since *within the phenomenological standpoint* we cannot presuppose the existence of the world but only our experiences of the world, we cannot assume the validity of any theory which for its verification requires the naïve acceptance of the existence of the world, which acceptance is implicit in the natural attitude. The upshot of this conclusion is that the phenomenological conception of evidence is unscientific, not in that it contradicts the definition of evidence as employed in the empirical sciences, but in that it is *prescientific*. The empirical scientist (conceived as a realist) uses evidence to further the growth of his theoretical knowledge about the world; the phenomenologist uses his own type of evidence in part in order to further his knowledge of *what it means* to be aware of the existence of the very world which the scientist, in his investigations, has presupposed. Were the empirical scientist to examine, as many do, what constitutes his belief in this world which, as scientist, he investigates, he would then be on the border of a phenomenological investigation.

Again I must emphasize that the phenomenologist is not a skeptic nor is he a phenomenalist. He does not either question or deny the existence of the world; he does, however, emphatically inquire into the nature of that evidence in experience on the basis of which we posit or believe in the existence of the world. Obviously the search for this evidence can only take place within the phenomenological standpoint since within the natural attitude the evidence available would relate only to the matter-of-fact characteristics of the world, the existence of which is already presupposed.

The difficulty in grasping the phenomenological conception of evidence partially explains Husserl's insistence, in the quotation at the beginning of this chapter, on the need to set aside previous habits of thought. It is my contention that this insistence, in conjunction with Husserl's point that phenomenology requires a new way of looking at things,[18] is no less than central to the understanding not only of Husserl but also of that greater part of contemporary existentialism which is phenomenological existentialism. Far too many discussions of existentialism, especially those with literary orientation, present a vitiated, often distorted, picture of existentialism precisely because of a failure to come to grips with an understanding of phenomenology and of its role, however qualified, in the works of the leading existentialists. The belief that these thinkers, especially Heidegger, Sartre, Ortega y Gasset, and Merleau-Ponty, can be successfully approached without some grasp of phenomenology is a myth. An overemphasis of Kierkegaard's irrationalism and an underemphasis of Husserl's phenomenology are among the chief reasons why existentialism, a strong force in the intellectual life of Europe, South, and Central America, has not yet achieved a position of philosophical respectability in the United States. It is unfortunate that too many students and interested laymen still receive much of their "understanding" of existentialism from professors of literature, religion, and fine arts and from literary critics and men of letters, instead of from professors of

[18] *Ideas*, p. 43.

philosophy in whose hands lies the proper responsibility for explicating the often technical points involved in a genuine understanding of existentialism.

A further point on the concept of evidence will both advance the explication and illustration of that concept and reintroduce the concept of the transcendental Ego as a point of departure for the continuing characterization of Husserl's phenomenology. Beginning with the concept of evidence, it is to be noted that Husserl distinguishes *adequate* evidence from *apodictic,* or absolutely certain, evidence. Evidence which is adequate is subject to greater and lesser degrees of comprehensiveness; for example, the evidence on which we base our implicit belief in the existence of the world gains in adequacy as the course of my experience continues to unfold along the usual lines; that is, objects continue to appear substantial, events continue to exhibit regularity in their behavior in such a way that prediction continues to be possible. However, should objects begin to take on hazy outlines and events become increasingly unpredictable (if not, in fact, impossible to discern because of the diminishing distinctness of objects), we might give up our usual belief in the existence of an external world altogether in favor of a belief in a world of "dreams." In other words, the belief in the existence of the world is based on evidence which may be more or less adequate, depending on the mutual consistency of our experiences of the world. The evidence for such a belief as this is, however, by no means apodictic, for it is possible, as I have done above, to entertain the possibility of the nonbeing of the world.[19]

An object given with apodictic evidence, on the contrary, is such that its nonbeing is absolutely unimaginable.[20] There is at least one object so given, the "I Am" of Descartes, the transcendental Ego of Husserl, which is itself the ground for all other judgments.[21] Having stated this point, Husserl is quick to note that although the *being* of the transcendental Ego (often called "transcendental subjectivity") is given in apodictic evidence, we do not, however, have fully adequate evidence of it. My transcendental subjectivity includes my past, for example, but this is available for present inspection only with the aid of memory, the evidence furnished by which is not apodictic.[22] Stated in a positive form, only the *living present* of

[19] *C. Med.,* pp. 14-16.
[20] *C. Med.,* pp. 14-16.
[21] *C. Med.,* p. 22.
[22] *C. Med.,* p. 22.

transcendental subjectivity is given in apodictic evidence; beyond the lived present, there extends a *presumptive horizon* (already alluded to above) which includes the Ego's past, its abilities as transcendental subject, and its habitual peculiarities.[23]

Looking out from the transcendental subjectivity instead of reflecting back on it, a different aspect of the presumptive horizon (in its relation to evidence) emerges: although my experience, within the phenomenological point of view, is describable as an experience *of the world,* the world *in itself* is not included within my experience. The existence of the world in itself has, in fact, been removed from relevance to the present discussion which pertains only to the phenomenological standpoint within which the judgment of existence or of nonexistence of common-sense objects is held in abeyance. Now, although the world is not within my experience, the fact that my experience is *of the world* requires further exploration.

In the first place, that my experience is of the world is not an isolated fact regarding my present experience, but is an instance of a general characteristic which *all* awareness has. Awareness is always awareness of something, even when the something in question is a negative fact such as an absence. This bipolarity of the relation of awareness to its object, that awareness is always *of* something, is termed by Husserl the *intentionality* of awareness;[24] it is that characteristic which makes an event in the stream of a consciousness different in kind from any other type of event.

In the second place, the fact that my perception is describable as being of the world (and this includes the perception of the world in a dream or delusion since these perceptions also can be reduced to the phenomenological standpoint and subsequently analyzed) serves to indicate, even though the existence of the world is not a fact within the phenomenological standpoint, that the sense of "of the world" is immanent within my perception. My perception, in other words, is not a mere configuration of data presented to awareness, although it does, to be sure, contain such data. It is a perception which has about it, in addition to data, the *sense,* the *meaning,* of

[23] *C. Med.,* p. 23. Although Husserl himself does not make this qualification in this context, it should be noted that the presumptive horizon that extends to what is not now experienced but may be meant has different modes; for example, the sense in which my past is included in a presumptive horizon is different from the sense in which the rest of my physical body not now present to my awareness is (e.g., my back).

[24] *C. Med.,* pp. 32-33.

being *of* the world. This meaning then is *in* my awareness, even though the object of the meaning, the world, is itself *not* within my awareness; from the point of view of my awareness phenomenologically conceived, the existence of the world is a *transcendent* fact with respect to which I make no judgment of acceptance or of non-acceptance. From this same point of view, however, the sense, the meaning of this transcendent fact is *immanent;* I know what it is to have an experience of the world—even in a dream when the "real" world is obviously not there. The point is that *immanent* in awareness is the sense of the *transcendent;*[25] and that simply because an object or event is related to awareness only as being included within the presumptive horizon of a transcendental subjectivity does not mean that its significance may not be operative within that subjectivity.

On the basis of this point rests the conception of *existence* which is central to understanding the existentialism of Martin Heidegger. When we come to him in our analysis, we shall see that his conception of existence rests on a reversal of this point. Heidegger states that the transcendental subject itself can transcend, can get beyond, its own subjectivity, thereby being actually out *in the world.* We shall see later that an analogous point is also developed by Husserl for whom it does not have full existential import because of Husserl's distinction between the transcendental Ego and the human Ego. The human Ego is an entity within the natural attitude; as such it is simply one object among many when viewed from the phenomenological standpoint. In this reduced capacity, the human Ego can no longer be regarded as *my self* in the full import of that term. It is primarily on the strength of this distinction made by Husserl between the transcendental Ego and the human Ego that Husserl himself failed to bridge the gap between phenomenology and existentialism, leaving that task to Heidegger, with his modified conception of phenomenology.

This last point is equally important and difficult. I shall therefore recapitulate it both for the sake of clarity and, incidentally, as a transition to the closing discussions in which Husserl's metaphysics of the relation of the human Ego to the world will be explicated. To the end of obtaining the most mileage possible out of this recapitulation, I shall develop it with reference to the distinction between the natural attitude and the phenomenological standpoint.

[25] *C. Med.,* p. 26.

These two notions may be redefined briefly by stating that the natural attitude is the common-sense way of viewing the world and our situation *in* it, and the phenomenological standpoint is the direction of our attention to *what it is* to experience a world and to be situated in it. In the phenomenological standpoint we suspend judgment with respect to the *real* existence of the world, neither affirming it nor denying it. In suspending this judgment with respect to the world, we also do so with respect to our bodies which are but items in the world; and we now direct our attention to *what it is to have a body*. Note that a phrase such as "what it is——" refers to an *essence*, a *characteristic*, rather than an existing state of affairs; the distinction between essence, what a thing is, and existence, that a thing is, is presupposed in this context. Generally speaking, in phenomenology the step known as *eidetic reduction* is just this attempt to capture and characterize the *essence* of anything given in evidence. The phenomenon is not the appearance itself but the general characteristic manifested by means of the appearance.

The crucial point is this: when I, for example, move from the natural attitude to the phenomenological standpoint, I cease to exist as a self inhabiting a body which I animate in virtue of the intimacy of my relation to it. I cease to exist in that manner because, in moving to the phenomenological standpoint, I have given up the fact of the existence of my body in favor of an awareness of *what it is to* exist as an embodied self. But I now see *what it is to exist as an embodied self* as the *essence* which it is. Phenomenologically, in other words, in the present example I exist as a transcendental Ego, an awareness of what it is to be an embodied Ego in the world. But it is just this embodied Ego, or at least an Ego essentially *engaged* in the world, not just a pure conscious subject, with which the existentialists are concerned. Thus Husserl's distinguishing between a transcendental Ego, pure conscious life as such, and a human Ego immersed in the world, and his granting of a primary reality to the former rather than to the latter, separate him in principle from the existentialists whom he has so strongly influenced.

What is significant about the distinction between the transcendental Ego and the human Ego is that Husserl's characterization of the human Ego in its relation to the world bears a striking resemblance to the existentialistic conception of human existence. In effect, the existentialists have rejected as untenable Husserl's conception of the disembodied pure consciousness which is the transcendental Ego; Heidegger asserts that human existence is essentially in the world, and Sartre explicitly denies the existence of a pure consciousness totally independent of reality. Prior to our detailed discussion of these other philosophers and their own employment of phenomenology, there remains one final task in regard to Husserl: the examination of the human Ego and its relation to the world.

The human Ego, or psychic life, is, as conceived by Husserl, what we grasp in internal experience,[26] that is, by introspection. This human Ego is always in the world; it is so from the point of view of each self as well as, for example, of the psychologist for whom the human Ego is an objective fact in the world which can be studied scientifically.[27] And in contrast to the disinterested onlooker that the transcendental Ego is, Husserl describes the human Ego as *immersed* in the world.[28] The metaphor of immersion here conveys the meaning of a deep engagement in the world, an interpretation corroborated by another passage:

> . . . human existence as such is always related consciously to an existent practical world as a surrounding world already endowed with humanly significant predicates. . . .[29]

And the mode of relatedness to this existent practical world is one of *intent;* Husserl asserts that the human Ego is *interested* in the world,[30] a quality which I underscore because of its similarity to the quality of care or concern (*Sorge*), to which Heidegger gives such a central position in his own philosophy.

Finally, since existentialists emphasize not just human existence but also the world, it should be noted that for Husserl the "humanly significant predicates" with which the world is endowed are constituted psychologically by the community of men who live in the world—a point that invites comparison with Nietzsche's assertion that it is we who have imposed value on the world, and who have created the world which is of concern to man.[31] This reference to psychological constitution in Husserl's later work gives evidence

[26] *C. Med.*, p. 25.
[27] *C. Med.*, p. 25.
[28] *C. Med.*, p. 35; cf. also p. 152.
[29] *C. Med.*, p. 135.
[30] *C. Med.*, p. 35.
[31] Nietzsche, *Joyful Wisdom*, pp. 235-236.

that the role of viewing in phenomenology was, Husserl's intention notwithstanding, being relegated to a position subordinate to the role of a subject who actively constitutes not only the meaning but also the being of the world:

> Every imaginable sense, every imaginable being, whether the latter is called immanent or transcendent, falls within the domain of transcendental subjectivity, as the subjectivity that constitutes sense and being.[32]

Fortunately for the course of existentialism, this aspect of Husserl's thinking never prevented him from *viewing* a great deal nor did it prevent him from developing in detail a method by which others could do the same.

[32] *C. Med.*, p. 84.

Heidegger: On Being in the World

4

And now suddenly, as soon as I left the others, I was conscious of being coerced no longer, and the world came to exist for me again, not as a foreign element to be looked at, but as a climate in which I could become immersed, whose parts were merely an extension of myself, or, the same thing, were continuous with me and I with them.

ALEXANDER TROCCHI, The Outsiders

It is unfortunate that philosophy, which should in principle be an unbiased search for the most fundamental types of truth, is not always the open-minded enterprise that its ideal nature requires. This weakness is painfully illustrated in the slow response often made by the philosophic community (if indeed any response is made at all!) to ideas introduced in the arts and letters. Were he to have done little else, which is emphatically not the case, it would still be to the credit of Martin Heidegger that he does not share with the philosophic community this professional mistrust of "imported" ideas. I say "professional" mistrust because most philosophers do read and enjoy novels and essays; too often, however, such reading fails to enrich in any essential manner their philosophical concerns.[1] Yet is it through the works of Heidegger (and also of Karl Jaspers, with whom this study does not deal) that the ideas of Kierkegaard and Nietzsche were funneled into the mainstream of

[1] Among those who could be mentioned as exceptions, an outstanding exception is Maurice Natanson, whose writings and lectures reflect extensive enrichment from the field of literature.

academic Western philosophy to the extent that professors of philosophy have been willing to widen the scope of topics considered philosophically respectable.

It is not readily apparent to the person beginning to read Heidegger's *Being and Time* that the book shows a heavy reliance on the works of Kierkegaard. At first, this book appears to be the usually technical treatise that would reasonably be expected from a disciple of Edmund Husserl. Heidegger, who was for some time assistant to Husserl, professed in his major work to be perpetuating the method of phenomenology as that method which permits the investigator to get *to the things themselves.*[2] Husserl, in stating that by means of phenomenology we do get to the things themselves, had taken the object of phenomenology to be the grasping of the *essential* character of the Ego and its experience of the world as against the scientific study of the *empirical* character of the world which includes, among other things, human Egos intimately related to living bodies. Heidegger as philosopher—in contrast to Heidegger as existentialist, the role in which he is being considered in this study—is unable to take phenomenology *just* as an investigation of essential characteristics of the Ego and experience because it is his intent to reawaken the problem of the meaning of Being itself, traditionally the fundamental problem of philosophy, especially of ontology. Phenomenology, in other words, as conceived by Husserl identified Being only with *essential* being, that is, the *universals,* the general qualities which are capable of being inherent or ingredient in particular things or events.[3] But to deal only with essential character is, as Husserl was fully aware, to leave outside consideration the question of existence and of nonexistence.[4] Indeed, the purpose of achieving the phenomenological standpoint was to do just that, to suspend the judgment of reality or nonreality in order better to inspect the essential characteristics of our experience of the world, which characteristics were considered by Husserl to be subject to analysis by a community of researchers. Heidegger chooses to widen the scope of phenomenology so that the question of reality and nonreality can come under its consideration. Although Husserl had addressed himself to that question on occasion,

[2] Martin Heidegger, *Sein und Zeit,* 9th edition (Tübingen: Max Niemeyer Verlag, 1960), p. 27. This reference hereafter cited as *SZ.*

[3] Husserl, *Ideas,* p. 44.

[4] As noted at the end of the last chapter, Husserl eventually contradicted himself on this point. Our considerations here are limited to his earlier position.

his treatment of it was limited to such problems as the appearing and nonappearing of evidence; Heidegger addresses himself to this question at the level of the inquiry into Being itself.

The nature of Heidegger's researches regarding the meaning of Being goes well beyond the scope of this study, but two subsidiary aspects of his investigations do not. The first is that the phenomenon to be described and analyzed is no longer the general character exemplified in an experience but is now defined as *that-showing-itself-in-itself,* the evident.[5] The *evident,* would, at first glance, appear to correspond to what Husserl meant by evidence, the *itself-given.* However, and this is a most important qualification, evidence for Husserl was primarily what was acquired *within* the suspension of the judgment of existence that obtains within the phenomenological standpoint. Heidegger does not make this suspension of the judgment of existence; therefore, the phenomenon for him, the showing-itself-in-itself, is not (metaphorically speaking) torn from its roots in Being itself.

Now by emphasizing the fact of the givenness of the phenomenon itself rather than the general quality ingredient in it, Heidegger is effectively, if not intentionally, opening the door to an element of subjectivism in *one sense:* namely, in the sense that the phenomena that *show themselves* to one person need not necessarily show themselves to another. The granting of this point entails the significant consequence that the findings of two phenomenological existentialists need not be in agreement with each other. The reports of an existentialist, in other words, need not be expected to hold in all respects for all human beings at all times.[6] I emphasize this point particularly because of the theoretical compatibility that it makes possible between the emphasis on the uniqueness of the individual in existentialism and the *de facto* uniqueness exhibited in the description of existence recorded by the existentialists themselves.

The second point of concern to us in Heidegger's re-asking of the question of Being is his statement that the fundamental ontological investigations must be pursued in the existential analysis of the Person.[7] The reason for this close connection between fundamental

[5] *SZ,* p. 28.

[6] This view has received its strongest statement in William Earle's "Phenomenology and Existentialism," *The Journal of Philosophy,* LVII, No. 2 (January 21, 1960), pp. 75-84. It may be noted also that Earle here states that phenomenology and existentialism are incompatible, a position relevant to our point at hand.

[7] *SZ,* p. 13. Heidegger's term *"Dasein"* will be translated as the "Person."

ontology and the Person can, in a limited way, be seen in the literal translation of the term which Heidegger employs to designate the Person, "being-there" (*Dasein*). The term "being-there" certainly illustrates what Heidegger intends for us to accept as philosophical truth, the implication of Being itself in the Person.[8] In the course of this study of Heidegger, it will be evident that this is but one of several ways in which Heidegger asserts the *essential relatedness* of the Person to what is other than itself.

Another aspect of this other-relatedness is grounded in Heidegger's definition of existence (*Existenz*), the essence of the Person.[9] The peculiar meaning which he gives this term *Existenz* presents a major difficulty in understanding Heidegger and is a cause of many misinterpretations of his philosophy. *Existenz* is to be distinguished from the traditional meaning of existence as the correlative of non-existence, that pair being parallel in meaning to being and non-being. When his intended meaning is being as opposed to non-being, Heidegger uses the Latin *existentia,* reserving, as I have noted, the German term *Existenz* for the essence of the Person.

Heidegger's definition of "existence" (*Existenz*) builds on the fact that, according to Heidegger, human reality is essentially *a being towards.* As such, its essence, termed "existence," must always be grasped as *a standing out from its being.* An etymological note will be helpful in deciphering how the essence of the Person can be a standing out from itself. The word "existence" comes from the Latin *existere* which means to stand forth, to arise.[10] By using the word "existence" in this etymological sense instead of with the sense of "being," Heidegger is characterizing the Person as that which can, in various senses to be specified in the course of this discussion, get beyond itself, can transcend itself.

This notion of self-transcendence is not new in the context of this study, for we have already seen that it was in effect employed by Husserl when he spoke of the human Ego as immersed in a world in which it was interested. The state of *being interested* is one of the

[8] *SZ,* p. 13. Heidegger's view that the Person is essentially related to being may have historical antecedent in Kierkegaard's notion that the human self is grounded in the power which constituted it—that is, God. Sören Kierkegaard, *Sickness unto Death* (Garden City, N. Y.: Doubleday & Company, Inc., 1955), pp. 146-147.

[9] *SZ,* p. 42.

[10] This explication is made by Werner Brock in his edition of Martin Heidegger's *Existence and Being* (London: Vision Press, Ltd., 1956), in footnote #14, p. 396.

ways in which a person can be self-transcendent, because the state of interest is a state *of the subject* that is interested, but a state which can only be completely understood in the *vector quality,* the directionality or thrust, that the interest has with respect to the object of the interest. In other words, interest is both *in* the subject who is interested and *in* the object of the interest: "I *have* an interest *in* that photograph." Interest, as well as other states of awareness, in virtue of being a state of awareness, shares the quality of *intentionality* which all awareness has, the state of being awareness *of* something. It is on the understanding of this *of*-quality of the state of awareness generally that the understanding of Heidegger's concept of existence rests.[11]

This characterization of the Person as one whose essence lies in his existence is still deficient with respect to Heidegger's over-all plan for defining the Person. The deficiency lies in the fact that Heidegger is concerned not only with defining the Person positively but also in denying the validity of other definitions that have hitherto had a wide acceptance, especially since he seems, on occasions, to feel that these invalid definitions have been attributed to him.[12] Heidegger states in *Being and Time*:

> The Person is no thing, no substance, no object.[13]

He also expresses agreement with Husserl in the latter's insistence that the unity of a Person is essentially different from that of natural entities.[14] It belongs to the nature of a Person to *exist* in the execution of *intentional acts;* thus it cannot be essentially objective.[15] We might note in passing that the disparaging meaning given to the notion of object in this context can, as in the case of the notion of existence, be explained etymologically; an object is what is *thrown against;* that is, it is something substantial, and therefore essentially unlike a person.

This agreement with Husserl is by no means complete, for Heidegger is unwilling to define the Person as consciousness itself,

[11] Martin Heidegger, "The Way Back into the Ground of Metaphysics," *Existentialism from Dostoevsky to Sartre,* pp. 214-215. Here Heidegger indirectly treats intentionality as in some sense derivative from existence.

[12] "The Way Back into the Ground of Metaphysics," pp. 213-215.

[13] *SZ,* p. 47.

[14] *SZ,* pp. 47-48.

[15] *SZ,* p. 48.

Husserl's definition of the pure Ego.[16] Heidegger is trying explicitly to bring about *a new experience of* the Person, one which will be adequate to one of Heidegger's ultimate concerns, the understanding of the involvement of Being in the Person.[17]

Nor should the nature of the Person be taken to be selfhood. Heidegger grants that being a self may be a feature of that which exists, a Person, but existence is not the same as selfhood. Here Heidegger's point is that in metaphysics the notion of selfhood is comprehended in terms of substance; that is, in terms of a substratum of personality:

> . . . something which maintains itself as identical in change of behavior and experience, and which yet refers itself to this multiplicity.[18]

This characterization of the Person as a substantial subject is not entirely illegitimate, since according to Heidegger it does function as a clue to the proper structure of the Person as Care (*Sorge*).[19] Later in the discussion of Care we shall see in what the unity of the Person does consist; in the meantime, it will be necessary to consider one of the major corollaries of Heidegger's thesis that to exist, to stand out beyond himself, is the essence of the Person. In this case the standing out of the Person is taken in its relation to the world; for Heidegger the Person is, as essentially standing out into the world, a being-in-the-world,[20] a characterization which might have pleased Nietzsche, despite its metaphysical context.

The hyphenated form of the phrase "being-in-the-world" is not intended merely to add to philosophical jargon, although it certainly has had that effect, as a look at some recent publications in psychiatry, for example, will attest. It is meant to emphasize that to be in the world, in the primary meaning which this notion is to have in Heidegger's analysis of existence, does not mean to be physically contained in the universe. On the contrary, being-in-the

[16] Husserl, *Ideas,* p. 113.

[17] "The Way Back into the Ground of Metaphysics," p. 213.

[18] *SZ,* p. 114.

[19] *SZ,* pp. 113-115. Heidegger's choice of the term "Care" affords a striking comparison with Alfred North Whitehead's description of an occasion of experience as having a *concern* for the object of experience. Whitehead, *Adventures of Ideas* (New York: The Macmillan Company, 1954), p. 226. Also worth noting is William James' treatment of the phenomenon of interest in his *Psychology.*

[20] *SZ,* p. 52 ff.

world is a "unitary *phenomenon,*"[21] and I have here reversed Heidegger's use of italics in order to emphasize the fact of the phenomenality of the object referred to by the phrase "being-in-the-world." *As* phenomenon it is the proper subject for study in *Being and Time.*

The immediate analysis of the concept of being-in-the-world yields the three obvious components: the world, the being who is in the world, and the relation *being-in* itself.[22] Since the *who* (who is in the world) is the Person—the implicit or explicit subject of most of this chapter, and explicated in the later analysis of Care—I shall discuss only the concepts of the *world* and the relation of *being-in* itself.

The *world* is *not* the world of things that are at hand, the things which, by virtue of their objectivity, a Person is *not.* Rather, the world is, in a sense to be specified, an aspect of the *Person himself.*[23] Viewing the world as an aspect of the Person may appear to us as a queer notion; this reaction reflects in part the fact that when we think about the world and attempt to capture just what we mean by the world, our tendency is to *objectify* the world, to view it as the spatially extended physical out-thereness. This out-thereness, however, is the world of objective thinking, the world of the historian, the geographer, and the astronaut. What concerns Heidegger in this context is not the physical world but the phenomenon, the world, which gives itself to us as an immediate component of our basic situation, being-in-the-world. The world is that in which the Person lives;[24] as such there are various possibilities:

> World means the "public" world of "ours" or the [that is, our] "own" and closest (domestic [that is, the one at which we are "at home"]) environmental-world."[25]

There remains a problem mentioned but not solved in introducing Heidegger's concept of the world, namely, the sense in which the world can be considered an aspect of the Person. Heidegger's in-

[21] *SZ,* p. 53.
[22] *SZ,* p. 53.
[23] *SZ,* p. 64.
[24] *SZ,* p. 65.
[25] *SZ,* p. 65. The quoted passage without interpolations gives the reader a small sample of the prose that makes *Being and Time* a formidable instance of German philosophical style.

tent here is not a Berkeleyan idealism, according to which the existence of the world does not extend beyond its being perceived. It is not, in this context, so much the being of the world that concerns Heidegger as it is the form—or better yet, the significance—of its being. I say "significance" rather than "nature" to emphasize the fact that Heidegger is doing a phenomenological, not a scientific, analysis; his problem is to characterize the world as an aspect of our concrete being-in-the-world instead of as a terminus of the scientific enterprise. Stated in Heidegger's own phrase, the problem under consideration is not simply the world but the *worldliness of the world.*

The being of worldly entities can be considered as one with the being of the Person in the sense that entities can have a meaning in virtue of their being set in a *matrix of significance* determined by the concern over the world on the part of a Person (viewed as being-in-the-world). This matrix of meaning, essentially characterized by *relations of reference,*[26] constitutes the worldliness of the world.[27]

The problem at hand can be dealt with less abstractly by turning our attention to the concrete type of phenomenon that well illustrates Heidegger's conception of the relation of reference, namely, *utensils,* in the sense of whatever is of *use*. For Heidegger the *being* of a utensil goes on beyond the mere fact that it *is,* to include the totality of uses by means of which the utensil in question can manifest its character. Analogous to Heidegger's conception of the Person as a *being towards* is his conception of the utensil as a *something in order to;*[28] that is, it is an entity whose being is essentially *a being referred to*[29] some other being in a manner to be explained. The significance of a utensil is, in other words, grounded in the implicit reference that it bears to other utensils. Heidegger illustrates this point by means of the sum of "things" in a room. The room is given to the Person not as what is spatially between four walls but as a matrix of inter-referring utensils which constitutes the room itself as a utensil having implicitly in its own being a totality of uses including, for example, habitation.[30]

The Person's knowledge of the utensility of the utensil is gained by the actual manipulation and use of it rather than by directing

[26] *SZ,* p. 151.
[27] *SZ,* p. 87.
[28] *SZ,* p. 68.
[29] *SZ,* pp. 83-84.
[30] *SZ,* pp. 68-69.

his sight to it. Heidegger's point here is that manipulation and use, as we shall see later regarding moods and feelings, are not blind.[31] They constitute a legitimate form of vision, one which gives to the employer of the tool that adaptation to its implicit usefulness as *this* tool.

Finally, in closing the discussion of the relation of entities to the Person, we note Heidegger's statement that the constitution, the make-up, of the utensil which is grounded in one of its aspects in its reference to other utensils, must ultimately be understood as a *for the sake of* the being of the Person.[32] Utensil, Person, and utensility are all but links of a concatenation, but it is the Person who provides the *telos,* the end, with respect to which the relations of reference among utensils achieve a *total* significance.

The third factor of being-in-the-world is the relation of *being-in* itself, the manner in which the Person is "in" the world. In what is perhaps one of his most insightful analyses, Heidegger describes three basic structures or functions which constitute the manner of this *being-in.*[33] The first of these structures, *Befindlichkeit,* translated roughly as "self-encountering," Heidegger characterizes as the state in which the Person has been brought before himself and there encounters by the instrumentality of *mood*[34] the *there* which he occupies. This encountering of one's place is not to be construed as a finding or discovery having the positive characteristics usually implied by these terms. The Person encounters himself as *being located there,* but this encounter does not meaningfully include any evidence of the where from or the where to of the being of the Person,[35] a fact to which Pascal also directed his reflections.[36] This state of being in the world at a definite place, yet without there being a comprehension of *why this place,* is termed "thrownness" by Heidegger. The notion of thrownness effectively conveys the sense of finding oneself located in the world in a nondecipherable manner while, at the same time, still charged with the responsibility for one's being,[37] one of Franz Kafka's central themes.

[31] *SZ,* p. 69.

[32] *SZ,* p. 84.

[33] The third aspect of *being-in,* speech (Rede), defined as the articulation of understanding, will not be taken up for discussion here. See *SZ,* p. 160 ff.

[34] *SZ,* pp. 134-135.

[35] *SZ,* p. 135.

[36] "As I know not whence I come, so I know not whither I go." Blaise Pascal, *Pensées* (New York: E. P. Dutton & Company, 1958), p. 55.

[37] *SZ,* p. 135.

A second feature of Heidegger's discussion of self-encountering that is particularly important to the philosophy of existence is the fact that the Person's discovery of his *there* in the world is effected by his moods—literally by his "attunement"—by which moods the Person learns *how things are going for the Person.*[38] The belief that one's feelings and moods are ways of being attuned to one's situation in the world, while not alien to common sense (especially to certain religious mentalities), has never had widespread acceptance in either British or American philosophy. In these two areas of philosophy feelings have for the most part been quickly labeled "mere feelings" and rushed off to philosophical limbo. On the other hand, Hegel, whose rationalism has been a common target for all existentialism, had without misgiving asserted the cognitive significance of feelings; that is, that feelings are a legitimate, albeit low-level, form by which truth can be apprehended.[39]

Whether or not the role of feelings in the Heideggerian sense of modes of attunement to one's situation be taken up for more extensive debate by philosophers, Heidegger's position, at least, on this point is quite clear: since moods are figuratively states of attunement to a situation whose meaning thereby becomes open to us, they effectively provide for the first time a meaningful ground for self-orientation on the part of the Person.[40] To understand this, one might reflect on, for example, the feeling of fear and the way in which that feeling may throw a commonplace situation into a sharply discriminated perspective. Heidegger also notes that moods and feelings may function negatively to obscure a situation.[41] Just as a feeling of inevitability and resignation to circumstances on the part of an observer in the face of disaster may enable him to disentangle some positive factor from a disintegrating situation, so may the feeling of panic, in the same circumstances, merely cloud the situation and effectively prevent positive conduct. The feeling in question does not increase or lessen the perceptive power of the Person, a Person otherwise conceived as a spectator to a situation which is outside of him. On the contrary, the problem under consideration here is an aspect of the *unitary* structure, being-in-the-world. Two aspects of this structure separable only in analysis are the Person who is in the world and the relation of *being-in,* in this

[38] *SZ,* p. 134.
[39] Hegel, *Logic,* p. 33.
[40] *SZ,* pp. 136-137.
[41] *SZ,* p. 136.

case apprehended in the mode of self-encountering. It is therefore all-important to the understanding of Heidegger's position on this question to re-emphasize that the Person in question *exists,* that he transcends himself into the situation which is, within the polarity of the structure of being-in-the-world, being illuminated or obscured by his state of attunement to that situation.

A second mode of the relation of being-in is *understanding* (*Verstehen*). As stated at the outset of the discussion of the nature of the Person, Heidegger holds that the Person is a *being toward,* a notion which was then explicated in the discussion of existence as a self-transcendence on the part of the Person. Up to this point, we have dealt with the concept of existence only in relation to the world conceived as the encountered field of the objects of our concerns. In the discussion of *understanding* we now turn our attention to another aspect of existing, yet perhaps a more important one, for the Person always understands himself as a projection *out from* himself, a projection made possible by the fact that *to exist* is the essence of the Person.[42] But in this case, the existing in question is not toward the world as such, but is toward the Person's own possibilities. This ability to be concerned with his own possibilities is a distinguishing characteristic of the Person, a characteristic not shared by the mere things that populate the world.[43] Furthermore, the Person, in its very manner of being, *is defined as* a power-to-be.[44] Unlike Kierkegaard, for whom one's being (existence) was the only reality which could be known without being transformed into a possibility, for Heidegger the being of the Person *is* his possibilities.[45] However, these possibilities are not possessed by the Person in a manner analogous to the way which an object in the world has its characteristics, for the possibilities of the Person have to be chosen by that Person and may in fact be lost.[46] The Person projects himself toward his possibilities by means of his understanding, in that the understanding has that character by which the Person's being-in-the-world can be grounded in the uncovering of the Person as a power-to-be.[47] So much by way of abstract statement; exactly what are the role and significance of the understanding?

[42] *SZ*, p. 12.
[43] *SZ*, p. 42.
[44] *SZ*, p. 143.
[45] *SZ*, p. 42.
[46] *SZ*, p. 42.
[47] *SZ*, p. 145.

First, it is important not to confuse Heidegger's concept of understanding with that of thinking; the latter is something in which I can engage or not, but the former is, on the Heideggerian view, a structure of the way in which I am in the world. It is equally important not to make the parallel error of taking the concept of projection to mean something on the order of making plans for the future; the same reason obtains in that I may make plans for the future or I may not, but projection is a structure of my being in the world. However, it is *relevant* to put aspects of each of these two points together in the following question: how is it that I can think about the future to the end of making plans for it? In other words, what is presupposed in thinking discursively about future activity?

The answer to this question lies in the projective character of understanding, which is to say: as a Person I am a being-in-the-world with all the intimacy of relatedness to the world intended by the use of that hyphenated phrase. There are occasions, however, in which I may, in effect, regard my being-in-the-world not as the self-involving phenomenon that it really is, but as an instance of almost physical containment. For example, in order to avoid the anxieties occasioned by the threat of an impending world war, I might let my life sink to a near vegetative form. Yet for the most part, this is not the case. Generally I see myself, not as a thing among things, but as a source of possible actions, of possible self-determinations. But to see oneself as a source of possibilities, however vague and unformulated they may be, is, in some sense quite difficult to specify, to have seized upon the future, somehow to have placed oneself in the future in the mode of a-being-which-is-not-*yet-can-be,* as an as yet unrealized possibility. This *anticipating self-comprehension* constitutes the projective nature of understanding.

What makes this point difficult both to develop and to understand is the fact that the common sense concept of possibility has a definite connotation which is alien to Heidegger's conception of possibility but which tends to color our understanding of the latter. Common sense, based as it is on observation of the commonplace events in which objects are involved, views possibility not so much as an object's present state, but rather as a future state, *that which can be realized.* To understand the notion of possibility in relation to a Person conceived, as Heidegger conceives him, as a self-illuminating[48] power-to-be, it is necessary to transcend, by way of a radical

[48] *SZ,* p. 133.

transformation, the common sense conception of possibility. For one thing, inasfar as the Person is self-understanding, his possibilities, unlike the possibilities of mere things in the world, are on the one hand present (and presented!) aspects of his being, and on the other hand are given as somehow already there in the future, a situation made possible by the fact that the existing, the self-transcending, of a Person has a temporal as well as a "spatial" dimension. For Heidegger the existential future is not the not-yet-but-yet-to-be, but is an integral aspect of the Person grounded in the projective nature of the understanding.[49] We may question Heidegger's eliminating entirely the "not-yet" aspect of the future from existential time, which aspect he is willing to admit as a character of clock time. However, it does seem undeniable that the future of the Person insofar as it is an object of that Person's understanding is apprehended in a manner analogous to our understanding of the progressive tense.[50] That is, if the future were in some way only the not-yet, we would be lacking the primordial understanding of futurity in the absence of which we could not so much as understand the meaning of the not-yet. For example, without some structure at least analogous to Heidegger's conception of understanding, how could we even think—since the process of thinking, although an event, typifies an event in which we are never merely *at one* point but which somehow always still involves us with what has gone before and meaningfully predisposes us to what is yet to come? In reasoning toward a conclusion, is not the existence *in the future* of the conclusion *now* one of the effective forces in directing the reason? Futurity, I submit, has no meaning unless the projective nature of the understanding be granted; the self, metaphorically speaking, is *spread out in time.*

A final note to conclude these reflections on the nature of temporality will also prevent the misconception that the future is the only phase of time with which Heidegger deals. Briefly, just as the projection of possibilities by the understanding constitutes the existential future of the Person, so the acceptance of his thrownness constitutes the authentic *past* of the Person. My past is not constituted by the now's that are no longer, but by what I *was then,* my given situation.

Future and past are not disjointed, however; I assume my past

[49] This is an interpretation of Sections 31, 32, *SZ,* pp. 142-153.

[50] For this point I am indebted to my wife.

on the occasion of looking forward to the future. I project my possibilities on the ground of my given situation, and it is in projection that it becomes necessary to assume my past *as* such a ground.[51] As for the present, its existential meaning is constituted by my confronting in their usefulness the things now at hand, those things that have been *present*-ed to me by the projection from a given situation.[52]

In the discussion of Heidegger's philosophy, we are now at a point at which the concept of freedom can meaningfully be introduced, for the Person has now been defined as a power-to-be whose self-comprehension projects his possibilities into the future. The freedom of the Person does not consist in a presumed state of indifference to these possibilities which he can be or fail to be. Rather, it consists in the fact that the Person—recalling here a characterization introduced earlier in this chapter—is *a being toward;* in this case, a being *toward* the most *authentic* exercise of his power-to-be.[53] In what does this authenticity consist?

Heidegger's conception of authenticity is not intended to have, by Heidegger's own statement (which can, of course, be called in question as it is by Sartre),[54] a connotation of ethical rightness or wrongness. Authenticity is stated to be nothing more than one of the possible ways of being in the world.[55] Ordinarily, our daily being-in-the-world, according to Heidegger, is inauthentic in that it is not under our own control:

> We enjoy and amuse ourselves as *One* enjoys; we read, see, and judge literature and art as *One* sees and judges. . . .[56]

This *One* who presides over our daily life is not this person or that person, nor is it *all* other people.[57] But still it is One who presents the appearance of doing our judging and deciding, thereby taking away responsibility from the Person.[58]

[51] *SZ,* pp. 325-326.
[52] *SZ,* p. 326.
[53] *SZ,* p. 144.
[54] Jean-Paul Sartre, *L'Être et le néant* (Paris: Librairie Gallimard, 1943), p. 122 (80). This source hereafter cited as *EN;* numbers in parentheses indicate corresponding pages from the English, *Being and Nothingness,* trans. Barnes (New York: The Philosophical Library, Inc., 1956). Translations here by the author.
[55] *SZ,* p. 129; p. 43.
[56] *SZ,* pp. 126-127.
[57] *SZ,* pp. 126-127.
[58] *SZ,* p. 127.

Although this mode of being, which Heidegger terms *inauthenticity,* is analogous to Kierkegaard's notion of being in *untruth,* there is an important difference between them. For Kierkegaard, to be in untruth by, for example, letting one's behavior "be determined by" one's being in a crowd, is to take a false view of the real situation; the real situation being that the individual in question is responsible for the very irresponsibility which he assumes as a guise by acting as a member of a crowd. Inauthenticity for Heidegger is not, however, a lesser mode of being.[59] In fact, it is a form in which the Person regularly keeps himself; it is the form of being which is "nearest" to the Person,[60] and it does not have the strong pejorative connotation that *untruth* has for Kierkegaard. For Heidegger the not-being-oneself, which the state of inauthenticity effectively is, is a *positive* possibility of a Person who has become too absorbed in taking care of affairs in the world as *one Person among others.*[61] Nevertheless, to be in inauthenticity is to be unfree, since the One is genuinely effective in making the Person's decisions. In view of this fact of unfreedom and also in view of the fact that inauthenticity is a normal form of daily life, how does a Person become free? How is authentic existence possible?

Clearly the answer to the problem of achieving authentic existence revolves around the discovery of a means, or at least an *occasion,* for disrupting the absorption of the Person who has fallen into inauthenticity. The Person, in virtue of his concern for the world, is in flight from himself[62] as an authentic power-to-be-himself. But Heidegger now adds, in a manner reminiscent of the gymnastics of theodicy, that the concealment of the Person's authentic possibilities from himself is only the *privation* of the correlative state, the openness to his understanding of these possibilities. In other words, to flee from one's possibilities presupposes an acquaintance with those possibilities. However weak this link in Heidegger's reasoning may be, the fact remains that the answer to the problem of freedom lies in discovering the occasion that calls us away from *doing as One does* to *doing as I choose to do.* This occasion is provided by the mood of *dread.*

In my opinion, there is one aspect in which Heidegger's discussion of dread makes a strong advance beyond what Kierkegaard had

[59] *SZ,* p. 43.
[60] *SZ,* p. 176.
[61] *SZ,* pp. 175-176.
[62] *SZ,* p. 184.

stated regarding that mood. Kierkegaard, whose *Concept of Dread* Heidegger has read and considers philosophically insightful,[63] had regarded dread as the mood that overcomes the individual confronting his freedom as a future possibility for himself. Heidegger, it seems to me, adds substance to the discussion of dread by grounding it relative to the *being-in-the-world* of the Person who experiences dread. Dread rescues the Person from inauthenticity by *setting him apart,* thereby breaking the hold of the One on him and freeing him for self-projection toward freely chosen possibilities. Differently stated, dread opens to the Person the (already presupposed) power-to-be-authentically, the power to choose freely what he is to be *by himself.*[64] This last phrase admittedly is open to two interpretations: the Person himself determines what he is to be in the world, *and* alone in the world the Person determines what he is to be. Both of these interpretations appear to be valid, but Heidegger's over-all discussion leaves little doubt that the latter best captures the essence of the situation:

> Dread sets apart and opens the individual as *solus ipse* [himself alone]. This existential "solipsism" is so little an isolated subject-thing in the harmless void of a worldless occurrence that [on the contrary] it brings the Person directly into an extreme sense ["awareness"?] before its world as world and with that it itself before itself as itself a being in the world.[65]

Heidegger's phenomenology of dread indicates here a much broader conception of the type of analysis to be conducted phenomenologically than what Husserl had outlined. Heidegger's phenomenology, in addition to being of such a nature as to permit its employment in ontological inquiry, is here being directed to what can be characterized only as a teleological subject matter: namely, the flight of the Person *toward* a concern with the "quiet familiarity" of things and *toward* being "at home" in the public mode of doing as One does. Inauthenticity is a movement for the sake of losing one's self by moving under the impersonal dominion of the One and is, by the same token, a movement away from the uncanniness of being thrown into the world charged with responsibility for oneself. Dread reveals this uncanniness; dread threatens, although

[63] *SZ,* p. 235, footnote.
[64] *SZ,* pp. 187-188.
[65] *SZ,* p. 188.

not necessarily explicitly, the Person who lives as One does. And the threat of dread can be there alongside the complete security of everyday concerns.[66] Kierkegaard had stated this point as forcefully as Heidegger, yet with considerably more fluency:

> And no Grand Inquisitor has in readiness such terrible tortures as has dread, and no spy knows how to attack more artfully the man he suspects, choosing the instant when he is weakest, nor knows how to lay traps where he will be caught and ensnared, as dread knows how, and no sharp-witted judge knows how to interrogate, to examine the accused, as dread does, which never lets him escape, neither by diversion nor by noise, neither at work nor at play, neither by day nor by night.[67]

But aside from the somewhat accidental feature of style, there remains Heidegger's often repeated insistence on the intimacy of relation between dread and one's being-in-the-world, an insistence perhaps Nietzschean in inspiration, that makes the concept of dread more generally relevant to philosophical and psychiatric discussion than had Kierkegaard's essentially theological treatment of it. But when Heidegger demonstrates that the relation between dread and being-in-the-world is twofold, only the absence of the theological coordinate makes his discussion significantly different from that of Kierkegaard's. Dread, for Heidegger, is a dread *of* being-in-the-world because of the uncanniness of the Person's being thrown into the world, but it is also a dread *for* being-in-the-world in that dread opens up to the Person the opportunity freely to exercise his power-to-be. Heidegger's point lacks originality when placed beside Kierkegaard's:

> For him [who knows well the possibilities of life] dread becomes a serviceable spirit which against its will leads him *whither he would go.* . . . Then when it announces itself . . . he does not recoil . . . Then dread enters his soul and searches it thoroughly, *constraining out of him all the finite and the petty,* and leading him hence whither he would go.[68]

Yet, unlike Kierkegaard who goes from his analysis of dread to a vague reference to faith,[69] as it was often his wont to do, Heidegger

[66] *SZ,* p. 189.
[67] Kierkegaard, *The Concept of Dread,* p. 139.
[68] Kierkegaard, *The Concept of Dread,* p. 142. Italics mine.
[69] Kierkegaard, *The Concept of Dread,* p. 139.

takes a rather bold phenomenological step by asserting that dread reveals the essential unity of the three aspects that make up the structure of the Person.[70] This total structure is termed Care (*Sorge*) by Heidegger almost as though to emphasize by the choice of the word the intimacy of relation between the Person and the world. Care, summarily stated, is composed of *existentiality* (being in advance of oneself), *facticity* (being in a particular situation in the world), and *fallenness* (being absorbed in the world). These three aspects can be explicated as follows:

The Person is a being that *goes to himself;*[71] this metaphor is understandable by reference to the earlier discussion of the projective nature of the understanding. I *am* the same Person that I *shall be* at some future date, but still I am *not now* that Person—in two different senses of the verb "to be," of course. In the sense in which I am not my future self, I *go to myself* in two senses, both relevant: with the passing of time I shall have reached (become) that self which is now temporally removed from me; and, also, I go to that self in that I project it as a possibility into the future *in order to* realize my present power-to-be. In either sense, and this is the first aspect of the Person, my self *is a being-in-advance-of-itself*.[72]

But Heidegger warns, with that emphasis that constitutes his hallmark, that this being-in-advance-of-itself is not an isolated tendency in a worldless "subject," a remark perhaps aimed at the early eighteenth-century German philosopher, G. W. Leibniz, who conceived of the universe as a totality of monads, self-enclosed subjects, each unfolding in its history certain innate and predetermined tendencies and including some equally prearranged perspectival representations which constituted the "world" for each monad. On the contrary, Heidegger's being-in-advance-of-itself is a being in the world in so integral a manner that *facticity,* the second aspect of Care, is an essential determinant of *existentiality.*[73] This facticity, introduced and analyzed briefly by Heidegger, although later developed in some detail by Sartre, is, I submit, one of the principal theses that modern philosophy ought to take up from existentialism for further discussion, whatever else be bypassed. One's situation is

[70] *SZ,* p. 191.
[71] *SZ,* p. 191.
[72] *SZ,* p. 191. This twofold connotation of the German *zu* [to] was brought to my attention by Mrs. Martha Husain.
[73] *SZ,* p. 192.

obviously a factor in the determination of the direction of one's life. But it is a different matter to argue, as Heidegger does here, that the situation *essentially* determines what the Person shall be by limiting the understanding's projection of possibilities into the future. Granting this point, the question of how an individual would have acted under different circumstances is no longer legitimate—it would *not* have been the same individual.

Finally, the third aspect of the unity of the Person is *fallenness,* a characteristic not without an interesting parallel in Husserl's statement that the human Ego is *immersed* and *interested* in the world. The meaning of *fallenness,* a suggestive term in its own right, lies in the Person's absorption in the world by virtue of his concern for it.[74] The choice of the term *fallenness* is obviously intended to imply the inauthenticity of too great an interest in the world with a consequent movement away from one's freedom.

In conclusion, the experience of dread reveals the unitary structure of the Person defined as Care as a being-already-in-advance-of-itself-in the-world-as-a-being-with-the-things-encountered-in-the-world.[75] We can now round out the problem introduced early in this chapter, the structure of being in the world: this total structure of Care is the fundamental structure of the being *who* is in the world.

Over and above the criticism of particular points and the consideration of the influence he has had in widening the scope of topics now considered respectable in academic philosophy, what sort of evaluation can be made of Heidegger's contributions? I propose two answers to this question.

In the first place, I suggest that Heidegger's philosophy is (in a respect quite similar to the philosophic contributions of John Dewey) a forceful, if not always either eloquent or clear, statement of the belief that man is not a creature apart but that he is, on the contrary, inextricably and essentially a participant in the world. The concept of existence as a standing out from oneself, the choice of being-in-the-world as the main structure of the Person, the emphasis on the inauthenticity of our everyday absorption in familiar things, and even the choice of the word Care as designating the totality of the Person—all of these factors bespeak the mind of a man who has listened carefully to Nietzsche's sermons on the meaning of the earth. It may be, as Heidegger writes, that the gods have

[74] *SZ,* p. 192.
[75] *SZ,* p. 192.

departed and that the world is darkening,[76] but the Heidegger of *Being and Time* is a man for whom *this* life in *this* world is good enough.

In the second place, although in my presentation I have excised as many as possible of those points made by Heidegger which appear to me to reflect primarily the peculiarities of his own personality, Heidegger's thought is nevertheless a curious intermixture of the methodical employment of the techniques of a modified phenomenology together with a highly personal, if not always original, view of life. It seems to me—and this is a view which I consider supported by the repeated use of quasi-theological terms and figures of speech in *Being and Time*—that Heidegger's philosophy can fruitfully be considered as an almost direct consequence of Kierkegaard's reduction of faith to the status of an absurdity. It is as though Heidegger saw that the next step in this dialectic would be to build a philosophy in which absurdity—the groundlessness of one's being in a particular situation—would receive a proper position, but without, at the same time, weighing down the metaphysics of that philosophy with the inclusion of a God rendered meaningless and, in practical matters, irrelevant by Kierkegaard.

[76] Martin Heidegger, *Introduction to Metaphysics* (Garden City, N. Y.: Doubleday & Company, Inc., 1961), p. 37.

Sartre (I): The Roots of an Existentialist

5

But there are people who are attracted by the durability of stone. They want to be massive and impenetrable, they do not want to change; where would change lead them? This is an original fear of oneself and fear of the truth.

JEAN-PAUL SARTRE, Reflections

Freedom is infinite and does not arise out of anything.

SÖREN KIERKEGAARD, The Concept of Dread

At what point does existentialism cease to be the exploration of fundamental structures of human existence and begin to be an almost literary documentation of the experiential vagaries of its author? I have already suggested, near the outset of the discussion of Heidegger, that the Heideggerian shift from an emphasis on the universal characteristic manifested in an experience to an emphasis on the experience itself in its concreteness makes possible *in principle* a situation which notoriously exists *in fact.* For with a shift from a concern with a general characteristic which in virtue of its generality could be proposed to another phenomenologist for analysis, it may be that this redefined phenomenology is not of the type that Husserl had envisaged; that is, a discipline to which various researchers could make positive and interlocking contributions simply by following the proper technique. With the shift to a concern with the phenomenon itself in its concreteness and the peculiarly personal context in which it is encountered—the individual existence—it seems only reasonable that the results of phenomenological researchers should take on a personal coloring.

By no means do I wish to suggest that the emergence of a personal flavor in phenomenological writings essentially weakens or invalidates them, nor do I wish to go to the other extreme represented by the spokesman for existentialism for whom there need be no common denominator *at all* between the existential descriptions of one author and those of another.[1] On the contrary, it seems to me, in spite of the personal coloring in the writings of existential phenomenologists, that there is in those writings a treatment of structures that can have, or even do have, a general validity transcending the limitations imposed on a research that uses for its materials only one's self and one's experience. Husserl thought that phenomenology, as he had developed it, successfully met the solipsistic difficulties that would seem to be implicit in a type of research that *begins* by suspending the judgment of existence in order to explore the structure of and the experiences had by the transcendental Ego. He polemicized philosophical anthropology, a precursor of modern existentialism, with its emphasis that ". . . true philosophy should seek its foundation exclusively in man and, more specifically, in the essence of his concrete worldly existence."[2]

Husserl's belief that phenomenology suffered from no such limitations as a ground in "concrete worldly existence," appears, when viewed from an existentialistically sympathetic perspective, as perhaps noble, but certainly vain. Such belief illustrates the type of position that Kierkegaard may have had in mind when he wrote:

> However, the objective way deems itself to have a security which the subjective way does not have . . . ; it thinks to escape a danger which threatens the subjective way, and this danger is at its maximum: madness. . . . The objective truth, as such, is by no means adequate to determine that whoever utters it is sane; on the contrary, it may even betray the fact that he is mad, although what he says may be entirely true, and especially objectively true.[3]

[1] The writer in question is William Earle who argues that ". . . there can be no essential *doctrine* of which among the infinite possibilities open to us is *really* our essential or authentic nature." ("Phenomenology and Existentialism," p. 79.) Earle's assertion here does not deny the point that there may be essential structures held in common by different individuals.

[2] Edmund Husserl, "Phenomenology and Anthropology," *Realism and the Background of Phenomenology,* ed. Chisholm (Glencoe, Ill.: The Free Press, 1960), p. 129.

[3] Kierkegaard, *Concluding Unscientific Postscript,* pp. 173-174.

To suggest that there is madness in Husserl's beliefs regarding the possibility of a pure (nonanthropological) phenomenology is not, however, to criticize Husserl pejoratively; there is certainly room in philosophy for madness of the special type identified by Plato in a discussion of beauty, a discussion which can easily be seen as also applicable to truth:

> . . . when he sees the beauty of earth, [he] is transported with the recollection of the true beauty; he would like to fly away, but he cannot; he is like a bird fluttering and looking upward and careless of the world below, and he is therefore thought to be mad.[4]

If for Plato's notion of recollection of ideal beauty there be substituted Husserl's expectation of the systematic development of phenomenology, this passage states what may very well be the fundamental problem facing the legitimacy of the phenomenological enterprise as it was conceived by Husserl. What is at stake is the possibility of effecting the phenomenological reduction from the natural attitude to the phenomenological standpoint, at which place there remains, in principle, for analysis only the transcendental Ego, its contents, and their transcendent significance. If *this* reduction is not possible, whatever else may be accomplished phenomenologically, then the phenomenologist in his researches is still *this* particular human being. In effect, if the phenomenological reduction of the human Ego to the transcendental Ego is impossible, phenomenology collapses (?) into existentialism, and the Husserlian hope for the establishment of phenomenology as a strict science, if not utterly defeated, is at least set back decisively on a major front.

Both Heidegger and Sartre effectively reject the possibility of the phenomenological reduction; they both, in their practice, are sympathetic to Kierkegaard's point that:

> The way of objective reflection makes the subject accidental, and thereby transforms existence into something indifferent, something vanishing. . . . the existing subjectivity has vanished, in that it has made an attempt to become what in the abstract sense *is called subjectivity,* the mere abstract form of an abstract objectivity.[5]

[4] Plato, "Phaedrus," *The Dialogues of Plato,* trans. Jowett (New York: Random House, 1937), u.p. 249.

[5] Kierkegaard, *Concluding Unscientific Postscript,* p. 173. Italics mine.

From the Kierkegaardian point of view, Husserl's rejection of philosophical anthropology in his phenomenology constitutes an instance of objective reflection; existence, for Husserl, is a matter of indifference, prevented from playing a role in phenomenological researches. For Heidegger and Sartre, however, reflection is subjective and existence, far from vanishing, is the object of the highest interest; one should, in evaluating either of these two figures, *make ample allowance for those aspects of their philosophies which reflect only the peculiarities of their own existence and no more.* I have enclosed this statement of the relation between phenomenology and existentialism in this chapter on Sartre because I feel that he, more than any other existentialist, has been frequently and viciously attacked by critics whose arguments are too often *ad hominem*—not intentionally so, but simply because they have failed to see that Sartre's phenomenology not only can but *should reflect* the morbidity of Sartre's existence if it is a fact that his existence is morbid. Furthermore, there is no inconsistency whatsoever between the morbidity reflected in Sartre's writings and the possibility of his genuinely illuminating certain structures of human existence. In my discussions, I am admittedly, as I was in the case of Heidegger, concerned with the analysis of the structures of human existence rather than with the more tabloidal aspects of Sartre's thinking that have frequently been unduly exploited. Those elements do not invalidate the possible relevance of Sartre's findings to the attempt to analyze human existence *in general,* a task which Sartre considered himself as performing.[6] Such analysis of human existence in general is un-Kierkegaardian, but on the validity of it rests the possibility of phenomenological existentialism as a legitimate philosophical discipline.

To begin the discussion of Sartre, let us examine a little-known monograph entitled *The Transcendence of the Ego: Outline of a Phenomenological Description,* published by Sartre in 1936 and 1937. Although compact and technical, *The Transcendence of the Ego* is written in a style which is clear in comparison with the verbal paradoxes of Sartre's major work, *Being and Nothingness.* Also, its point of departure is in part a disagreement with a specific passage in Husserl's *Ideas,* a passage which provides an excellent foil against which Sartre can state his own position.[7] Finally, in spite of

[6] Sartre, *EN,* p. 533 (456).

[7] Jean-Paul Sartre, *The Transcendence of the Ego,* trans. Williams and Kirkpatrick (New York: Noonday Press, 1937), p. 114, fn. #46. This reference hereafter cited as *TE.*

the statement of a philosophical position which is close in *form* to a Husserlian phenomenology, there is in *The Transcendence of the Ego* a Kierkegaardian insistence on the nature and extent of human freedom, an insistence which will, during the course of his philosophical and literary career, become a virtual hallmark of Jean-Paul Sartre.

The Husserlian passage to which Sartre addresses his critical remarks occurs, as I have indicated, in Husserl's *Ideas.* Husserl introduces his thesis regarding the status of pure consciousness as a system of "Absolute Being," a thesis explained in Chapter 3 of this study. However, after stating his thesis, Husserl makes a later statement which involves a subtle but important change in the position. This change, if weighted heavily in interpreting Husserl, can lead to the conclusion that for Husserl consciousness is never actually *pure* consciousness, for it is always, even after the phenomenological reduction, *inhabited* by the pure Ego. And it is upon this later statement that Sartre directs his criticism, for Husserl has said:

> . . . we will count the pure Ego as a phenomenological datum only so far as the immediate and clearly ascertainable peculiarity of its essential nature reaches, and *it is given together with* pure consciousness. . . .[8]

Husserl's point here, as Sartre sees it, is that the Ego (or "I" as Sartre usually terms it) is being granted a permanence that transcends the purity of consciousness as such.[9] The phenomenological reduction as performed by Husserl, in other words, is not complete; a special dispensation has been granted to the *existence* of the Ego in spite of the fact that *all* judgment of existence is supposed to have been suspended on the occasion of performing the phenomenological reduction:

> If the *I* in the *I think* affirms itself as transcendent, this is because the *I* is not of the same nature as transcendental consciousness.[10]

Some of the problems with which this realization leaves Sartre are: In what way is the Ego "presented to" consciousness? What is the nature of the Ego? What relation obtains between the Ego and consciousness? How is consciousness to be characterized if the dis-

[8] Husserl, *Ideas,* p. 173. Italics mine.
[9] *TE,* p. 50.
[10] *TE,* p. 51.

tinction between it and the Ego is granted? Finally, in what way does the concept of freedom have to be formulated since consciousness is now being conceived as *radically other than* the Ego, which is now said to transcend rather than to inhabit consciousness? The following discussion of *The Transcendence of the Ego* will show (although not necessarily with the discreteness suggested by the *listing* of the questions) how Sartre deals with these problems.

For Husserl, the Ego, while belonging to every experience in a stream of consciousness, was not one experience among others in that stream,[11] nor, for that matter, would it have been one of the objects *of which* there are experiences in the stream of consciousness. For Sartre, however, the Ego is an object of which we are aware, subject to an essential qualification: the intuition of the Ego as an object of consciousness is possible only on the occasion of a *reflective act* on the part of consciousness.[12] To expand on an example used by Sartre: when one is engaged in reading, there may be a consciousness of the book as an object or perhaps of the quality of the paper and the style of the type; on other occasions, describable by saying "I am engrossed in the book," there may be a consciousness of the events or of the drama of the events depicted in the book. But there is no I, no Ego, inhabiting this consciousness. The book, the quality of the paper, the drama of the events, and other items are present to consciousness but not the Ego:

> There is no place for *me* on this level. And this is not a matter of chance, due to a momentary lapse of attention, but happens because of the very structure of consciousness.[13]

The Ego is given *through* reflective consciousness with evidence, although this evidence is neither apodictic nor adequate.[14] The Ego is given as an existent,[15] and moreover as an existent that transcends the reflective consciousness to which it is given.[16] As a transcendent existent it is, contrary to Husserl's position in the *Ideas,* subject to phenomenological reduction.[17] But the existence of the Ego is not

[11] Husserl, *Ideas,* p. 172.
[12] *TE,* p. 53.
[13] *TE,* p. 49.
[14] *TE,* p. 51.
[15] To speak of the Ego here as an existent is only to say that it *is* rather than that it *exists* in the Heideggerian sense.
[16] *TE,* p. 52.
[17] *TE,* p. 53.

self-subsistent; on the contrary, it is (and here Sartre is employing the constitutive version of phenomenology outlined at the end of Chapter 3) an existence constituted by the activity of consciousness in a manner analogous to the way in which consciousness constitutes, or may fail or *refuse* to constitute, the beauty of a symphony. Just as the beauty of a piece of music depends on the activity of an aesthetically oriented constituting consciousness, so also does the existence of the Ego which is constituted as the ideal pole for states and actions.

To clarify this last point let us look back briefly at Husserl's *Cartesian Meditations,* from which Sartre appears to have borrowed the concept of polarity. Husserl conceived of the Ego as continuously constituting itself not only as *this* continuous stream of awareness but also as, at the same time, the same I.[18] The Ego in its capacity as this personal identity underlying the flow of experience Husserl referred to as an identical pole of the subjective process. In the passage of Sartre's under consideration, the Ego is said to be the pole of states and actions; the Ego is the synthetic (in virtue of its constitution by consciousness) totality of its states and actions, of its love and hate and of its playing a piano or driving a car. To specify that this pole is an *ideal* pole is intended by Sartre to cover the fact that the Ego is *no more than* its states and actions synthesized into a totality, although the Ego is not reducible to *an action* or *a state*.[19] Viewed with respect to its actions, the Ego is *I*; with respect to its states, *me*.[20]

Up to this point, Sartre's reflections on the nature and constitution of the Ego, although different in important respects from Husserl's treatment of that concept, have nevertheless been conducted only within the domain of phenomenology. But here it is now possible to introduce a teleological dimension into the analysis, following the precedent set by Heidegger in *Being and Time,* by asking: Why does consciousness constitute an Ego for itself? In answering this question, Sartre goes beyond a mere phenomenology to a Kierkegaardian philosophy of existence within a phenomenological framework. The touchstone for the transition is the characterization of the essence of consciousness after Sartre's repudiation of Husserl's belief that consciousness was by nature *personal* because of the intimacy of its relation to the Ego that inhabits it. If in theory the

[18] Husserl, *Cartesian Meditations,* p. 60.
[19] *TE,* p. 74.
[20] *TE,* p. 60.

Ego be uprooted from its immanence in consciousness and if it subsequently be conceived as a transcendent object itself constituted by consciousness, then the Husserlian notion of a personal consciousness is replaced by a consciousness that is *impersonal,* or perhaps, to emphasize another relevant connotation, *prepersonal.*[21] The Ego is no longer the agent that constitutes the identity of *this* consciousness; rather, it is the spontaneity of consciousness that makes possible the unity of the Ego.[22]

As to the unity of the consciousness, for Sartre (some contradictory statements notwithstanding)[23] that unity lies in the fact that consciousness is a perpetual synthesis of past and present consciousness; that is, that consciousness constitutes its own unity.[24] This *immanent* unity of consciousness is, however, to be clearly distinguished from the *transcendent* unity of the Ego, a unity also constituted by consciousness.[25]

How else can the transcendental field be characterized, over above its impersonal and self-unifying character? Here Sartre stands closest to Kierkegaard's statement that freedom is infinite and arises out of nothing,[26] as well as to Nietzsche's statement that it is a falsification of evidence to say that a subject "I" conditions the predicate "think." [27] In Sartre's words:

> . . . transcendental consciousness is an impersonal spontaneity. It determines its existence at each instant, without our being able to conceive anything *before* it. Thus each instant of our conscious life reveals to us a creation *ex nihilo.* . . . There is something distressing for each of us, to catch in the act this tireless creation of which *we* are not the creators.[28]

Sartre is here stating what is perhaps one of the most dramatic dilemmas in the history of philosophy. On the one hand, here is a strong affirmation of the existence of a spontaneity that transcends freedom, if by freedom we mean self-determination. On the other hand, the statement is at the same time an occasion for distress in that the spontaneity being affirmed is *not* anyone's spontaneity.

[21] *TE,* p. 36; pp. 96-98.
[22] *TE,* p. 40.
[23] *TE,* p. 38; p. 49.
[24] *TE,* p. 37; p. 60.
[25] *TE,* p. 60.
[26] Kierkegaard, *The Concept of Dread,* p. 100.
[27] Nietzsche, *Beyond Good and Evil,* p. 18.
[28] *TE,* pp. 98-99.

Insofar as consciousness is a spontaneity, Sartre's position here is saved from being a mere Nietzschean determinism according to which conscious states generally are "secretly guided" by the instincts and "forced along certain lines." [29] Nevertheless, Sartre's similarity to Nietzsche here is undeniable, although the similarity to Kierkegaard is even stronger, both in terms of the sheer lack of determination of any sort in the sphere of freedom and especially in the relation that is stated to hold between this freedom and our awareness of it.

But even this last statement contains a subtle distortion, for, as Sartre notes, what frightens consciousness (that is, "what occasions dread" in Kierkegaardian terms) is the fact that consciousness senses that this spontaneity is beyond freedom;[30] that is, it is beyond *self*-determination since the self is but a passive product of this very spontaneity of consciousness. Dread, termed here by Sartre "a vertigo of possibility," is understandable:

> . . . only if consciousness suddenly appeared to itself as infinitely overflowing in its possibilities the *I* which ordinarily serves as its unity.[31]

We have, in this passage, the embryonic form of Sartre's theory of self-deception as well as the evidence required in order to answer the question proposed earlier: why does consciousness constitute an Ego for itself? Sartre's answer is that consciousness constitutes the Ego as a false representation of itself in order to mask its own spontaneity from itself:

> . . . as if consciousness hypnotized itself before this ego which it has constituted, absorbing itself in the ego as if to make the ego its guardian and its law.[32]

In spite of this essentially negative role in which Sartre casts the Ego, he still sees in this phenomenology of the Ego a positive, and strikingly Heideggerian, contribution, that the phenomenologists have plunged man back into the world.[33] This new status of man has been effected by removing the Ego from the privileged position

[29] Nietzsche, *Beyond Good and Evil,* p. 3.
[30] *TE,* p. 100.
[31] *TE,* p. 100.
[32] *TE,* p. 101.
[33] *TE,* p. 105.

ascribed to it by Husserl in the transcendental field and by treating it as one existent among others in the world and as having the same essential characteristics as the world.[34]

A more original insight and eventually a more important one in relation to his major work is Sartre's point that the transcendental field of consciousness, purified of the existence of the Ego, is now seen to be *nothing:*

> . . . Since all physical, psycho-physical, and psychic objects, all truths, all values are outside it; since my *me* has itself ceased to be any part of it. But this nothing is *all* since it is *consciousness of* all these objects.[35]

Here we have a hint of what will, in *Being and Nothingness,* appear as a full-blown ontology arrived at by means of phenomenological techniques. Centrally located in this ontology is Sartre's phenomenological existential concept of a *nothing* which somehow *is,* yet *has no being.* We shall continue exploring this phenomenology of nothingness and its relation to self-deception after a brief consideration of Sartre's further delineation of the concept of freedom in his *The Psychology of Imagination,* for it is in his phenomenological study of the nature of images and the relations obtaining among images, consciousness, and the world that Sartre develops the notion of freedom as a separability *from the world* of a consciousness which is *in the world.*

In order to understand Sartre's thought regarding the imagination, it is necessary to examine first an aspect of Husserl's phenomenology, the *noetic/noematic* structure of awareness. According to Husserl, it is a fact that we can be aware of the same object in different ways, of different objects in the same way, and also of different objects in different ways. For example, with respect to the object, I can perceive a table, a pen, and a framed picture; with respect to the mode of awareness, I can perceive a table, I can imagine a table, and I can remember a table—in each case, the *same* table. Husserl termed the object of awareness the *noema* and the mode of awareness of the object, the *noesis.*[36] To understand Husserl's phenomenology on the problem of the imagination it is important to keep in mind that when I perceive *this* table or when I imagine *this* same

[34] *TE,* p. 105.
[35] *TE,* p. 93.
[36] Husserl, *Cartesian Meditations,* p. 36.

table, I am aware of the same noema in two different modes. Of course, the image of the table is *not* the table, but by means of my apprehending the image of the table I have a secondary apprehension of the table itself.[37] Sartre concerns himself with studying the essential difference between perception and imagination with respect to the modes in which each of these presents its object, rather than distinguishing as Husserl does between a primary and a secondary apprehension. The object of perception is posited as real; that is, the object perceived is, in virtue of its being perceived, taken to be a real object. But in the case of imagination either the object is posited as nonexistent, as absent, as existing elsewhere, or, in the neutral case, the object simply may *not* be posited as existing at all.[38] Thus the characteristic possessed by an image that distinguishes the image in essence from the object of perception is that, according to Sartre, the image ". . . involves a certain nothingness":[39]

> Alive, appealing and strong as an image is, it presents its object as not being. This does not prevent us from reacting to the image as if its object were before us. . . .[40]

Regarding this distinction between perception and imagination, Sartre makes two observations. The first is that, in the case of perception, the object perceived is given against a background of total reality;[41] the object is, as it were, the figure, and reality is the ground. The top of the desk now visible to me is part of the desk, itself part of what is in the room, and so on. In contrast to this mode of givenness of the perceived object is that of the imagined object. Instead of being given against the ground of the totality of the real, the imagined object is given (to take only one of the four possible modes listed above) precisely as absent,[42] which is to say, the imagined object is given as something which is *nothing* in relation to the background of real things.[43]

In virtue of this nothingness of an imagined object, it is necessary to take up the question: How is the nature of consciousness to be

[37] Husserl, *Ideas*, p. 37.

[38] Jean-Paul Sartre, *The Psychology of the Imagination* (New York: Philosophical Library, Inc., 1948), p. 16. This reference hereafter cited as *PI*.

[39] *PI*, p. 18.

[40] *PI*, p. 18.

[41] *PI*, p. 262.

[42] *PI*, p. 262.

[43] *PI*, p. 263.

construed so that it will be possible to understand how consciousness can posit an image; that is, how consciousness can bring before itself an object that is nothing in relation to the contents of reality? It is Sartre's contention that, if consciousness were but one event among others in the world, and if it were also in thoroughgoing causal interaction with these other events, that there could be no awareness of images *as* images, as representations:

> If we assume a consciousness placed in the very bosom of the world as one existence among others, we must conceive it hypothetically as completely subjected to the action of a variety of realities—without its being able to avoid the detail of these realities by an intuition which would embrace their totality. This consciousness could therefore contain only real modifications aroused by real actions and all imagination would be prohibited to it, exactly in the degree to which it would be engulfed in the real.[44]

Sartre's thesis is that, in order for an image to be entertained *as* an image, consciousness must set the image over against the totality of the real, since the image is not one real item among others but merely a representation. But, in order for the imagination to posit the image as over against reality, it is necessary that consciousness *not* be "engulfed in the real" and determined in all its aspects by the causal efficacy of reality upon it. Consciousness has to disentangle itself from reality in order to posit the image as a nothing in relation to the real, since, if such a disentanglement were not effected, the image could only be one other real item among others. As such, it would not be an image, but merely another item presented to consciousness because of the activity on consciousness of the other events that constitute reality. And it is just this ability to set itself over against the totality of the real that constitutes the freedom of consciousness:

> For a consciousness to be able to imagine it must be able to escape from the world by its very nature, it must be able by its own efforts to withdraw from the world. In a word it must be free.[45]

This freedom from reality, this escaping from the world, is conceived by Sartre as definable correlatively to a (Heideggerian) being-

[44] *PI,* pp. 266-267.
[45] *PI,* p. 267.

in-the-world.[46] In other words, consciousness can withdraw from the world on the ground of a logically prior being in the world. Consciousness, which has now been shown to be in essence imaginative, posits the image as a nothing *in relation to* the real in which consciousness is basically engaged but which, in virtue of its imaginativeness, it can transcend.[47]

The method of doubt employed by Descartes does apparently, then, have a certain priority which is more than merely methodological, for, according to Sartre, to apprehend doubt reflectively is to have an *apodictic* intuition of freedom.[48] In order to doubt, in order to question the real, the doubter has to set himself apart from the world. The world is that with respect to which there is doubt, and the doubter, in virtue of his very doubting, is seen necessarily as one who is free in his setting himself apart from the world and from the causal chains which would, in the absence of freedom, bind his consciousness. At the very same time, the fact of doubt illustrates the one structure of consciousness as a being-in-the-world since, were this not a basic structure of consciousness, consciousness could not exercise doubt—doubt being defined in terms of a questioning extrication of consciousness from reality.[49]

Implicit in the preceding discussions of imaginativeness as an essential aspect of consciousness there has been a distinction between the totality of the real, on the one hand, and the world, on the other. This distinction, which will reappear in *Being and Nothingness* as the distinction between Being and the World, illustrates that the concept of *meaning* for Sartre rests on his theory of the imagination and therefore on the nature of freedom. Although consciousness is a being-in-the-world, there is yet a sense in which the concept of the world is not fundamental but rather derivative from the fact

[46] *PI*, p. 269.

[47] *PI*, p. 269.

[48] *PI*, p. 270.

[49] Somewhat incidentally, this connection between the freedom of consciousness and its being-in-the-world is for Sartre the ground for explaining why there is no freedom on the part of the dreaming consciousness. (Sartre may here be factually wrong; others besides myself agree to the existence of dreams in which the dreamer undeniably has a hand in the unfolding of the dream-events. Such dreams occur, for the most part, on Sunday mornings.) The dream being a fiction, there is no being-in-the-world for which consciousness can extricate itself, such extrication being tantamount to exercising freedom. (*PI*, pp. 246-255.) Dreaming is akin to being engrossed in a vivid story, a story which, as the colloquialism aptly phrases the matter, *holds* the reader.

of the imaginativeness of consciousness. Simply stated, Sartre's point is that

> The imaginary thus represents at each moment the implicit meaning of the real.[50]

The real is what is *simply* there for awareness. Therefore, to apprehend the real *as world,* as a meaningful articulation of data, it is necessary that the real, the simply there, be surpassed toward the imaginary.[51] The sense of this notion of surpassing toward the imaginary is that the situation directly confronted *perceptually* receives a definition by having placed (metaphorically) alongside it an imaginative consciousness which is in an essential respect a reverse of the perceived situation.[52] For example, I note the absence of my dictionary *not simply* because the dictionary is not perceptually encountered in the bookcase, but also because the imaginativeness of my consciousness places beside what I *do* perceive in the bookcase the image of the dictionary, an image which presents the dictionary *as being absent.* The *real* is what I immediately confront; the *world* is that same situation, meaningfully articulated by the imagination and set over against the consciousness that is there engaged:

> . . . imagination, far from appearing as an *actual* characteristic of consciousness turns out to be an essential and transcendental condition of consciousness.[53]

As well as of *freedom* and the *world.* . . .

[50] *PI,* p. 272.
[51] *PI,* p. 273.
[52] *PI,* p. 272.
[53] *PI,* p. 273.

Sartre (II): A Handbook for an Overman

6

Then, as would appear, the opposition of a part of the other, and of a part of being, to one another, is, if I may venture to say so, as truly essence as being itself, and implies not the opposite of being, but only what is other than being.

PLATO, Sophist

Profane though this comparison will seem to some observers, the historical roles played by Thomas Aquinas and Jean-Paul Sartre have similarities that make it worth our while to put the philosophical contributions of these two figures alongside each other momentarily. Each man has come to be considered, in some circles, as *the* representative of his type of philosophizing. Aquinas suffered during his lifetime, as Sartre continues to suffer during his, extensive and bitter criticisms at the hands of contemporaries. Their most striking similarity, however, lies in the fact that both Aquinas and Sartre bound together into imposing monolithic structures many of the intellectual building blocks that were available to them in their time. And yet neither can be considered a mere craftsman in that the finished product in each case remains an undeniable work of original genius. Among the resources available for the Thomistic synthesis were the Judaic-Christian religious scriptures and traditions, and the philosophies, among others, of Plato, Augustine, Averroës, Avicenna, and especially Aristotle. The complexity of the materials included and transformed as he incorporated them in his thought is sufficient in itself to becry the shallowness of the still not uncommon assertion that Aquinas merely cast Christianity into an Aristotelian mold.

By the same token, a brief consideration of the materials available to and taken up for consideration by Sartre shows the injustice of asserting that Sartre's existentialism is an almost automatic result of a confluence of Kierkegaard's emphasis on subjective content and Husserl's emphasis on essential form. For example, and by way of anticipating some of the topics for discussion in this chapter, we find in Sartre's thinking:

a) Descartes' concept of the importance of doubt as a mode of relatedness to the world.
b) Kierkegaard's reflections on the individual, on freedom and dread, responsibility for oneself, and on the significance of time.
c) Nietzsche's involvement with the absence of God and its relation to the problem of values, his concern with the subject's interpretation of reality and the opening of horizons.
d) Husserl's phenomenology in a modified form in which the natural attitude constitutes an attempt to escape from one's freedom,[1] as well as Husserl's Cartesian emphasis on consciousness.
e) Heidegger's concepts of being-in-the-world and of transcending time by projecting possibilities, as well as his emphasis on facticity, freedom, and the relationship between essence and existence,[2] along with the cognitive significance of moods and feelings.
f) Hegel's convoluted, obscure, and ponderous manner of expression!

These contributions, taken in conjunction with Sartre's own belief in the radical otherness obtaining between human reality and the being on which it essentially depends, constitute a listing of those building blocks with which we shall be most concerned in approaching Sartre's philosophy.

In spite of an employment of phenomenology on the whole closer to Husserl's original intention than to the ontologically oriented version developed by Heidegger, the point of departure for the

[1] Cf. Sartre, *Transcendence of the Ego,* pp. 102-103.

[2] "Existence" as Sartre uses it refers to the Thomistic *existentia,* not the Heideggerian *Existenz.* That consciousness is capable of transcendence in virtue of its intentionality enables us to say of it that it also *exists* in the Heideggerian sense.

phenomenological analyses in Sartre's *Being and Nothingness* can be identified by Heidegger's term, being-in-the-world. Sartre's understanding of the concept of being-in-the-world is not, however, completely consistent with what Heidegger had intended by it. Whereas Heidegger had explicitly chosen to bypass consciousness as the defining characteristic of the Person who is in the world, Sartre, on the contrary, considers being-in-the-world as consisting of consciousness and the phenomena presented to it:

> The concrete [the basic fact] is man in the world with that specific union of man with the world which Heidegger, for example, terms "being-in-the-world." [3]

Sartre's characterization of this being-in-the-world is similar to Husserl's description of the *life world,* the surrounding practical world in which meaning has been endowed by the human beings in it.[4] For Sartre, in our immediate living in the world:

> This immediate[-ly experienced fact] is the world with its urgency.[5]

> Our being is immediately "in situation." . . . We discover ourselves in a world already populated with exigencies, in the midst of projects "in the course of realization." [6]

Thus in Sartre's view the world is not merely, as it was for Husserl, meaningful; it is demanding—*in its immediacy!*

The primary analysis of Sartre's being-in-the-world yields two factors: being-*for-itself* and being-*in-itself*. Although it is impossible to explicate either of these in complete isolation from the other, discussion in this chapter will be roughly divided into two halves. In the first, the doctrine of the for-itself and some of its more important corollaries will be presented; in the second, the same will be done for the in-itself.

Perhaps Sartre's doctrine of the for-itself can best be introduced in contradistinction to Husserl's definition of the transcendental Ego as a closed realm of Absolute Being, self-contained in its existence.[7] Although, like Husserl, Sartre conceives of the for-itself as

[3] Sartre, *EN,* p. 38 (3); see also p. 538 (460).
[4] Husserl, *Cartesian Meditations,* p. 135.
[5] *EN,* p. 76 (38).
[6] *EN,* p. 76 (39).
[7] Husserl, *Ideas,* p. 153.

consciousness, he nevertheless refuses to grant to consciousness a being *in itself*. Consciousness reveals being, but has no being of its own in the sense of self-subsistent being. Since consciousness is intentional, that is, since consciousness is essentially a consciousness *of* something, it follows that

> . . . for consciousness there is no being outside of that precise obligation to be an intuition revealing something, that is to say, of a transcendent being [the in-itself]. Not only does pure subjectivity fail to transcend itself in order to posit an objective, if it is given at first; but, more than that, a pure subjectivity vanishes.[8]

The fact of the intentionality of consciousness is, for Sartre, a sufficient consideration for the conclusion that consciousness, although it *is* in one sense, is by no means self-subsistent; that is, it cannot exist in and by itself. Rather, consciousness in its being is supported by a being which it is not; the intentionality of consciousness, in other words, is literally a constitutive structure of consciousness. If consciousness did not transcend itself to the being *of* which it is a consciousness, there would be no consciousness.[9] Instead of saying that there cannot be consciousness of nothing, Sartre would prefer to say that if consciousness were only of nothing, it could not be.

The intentionality of consciousness does offer a further clue regarding the nature of consciousness; for, if consciousness is an awareness *of* a being which consciousness is *not,* it may be that this function of *not being* that of which consciousness is an awareness may offer some insight into the character of consciousness. That the power of negation is essential to the human reality that is consciousness, Sartre finds implicit in Heidegger's conception of the Person (*Dasein*) even though for Heidegger consciousness was not a defining characteristic of the Person. Nevertheless, Sartre takes Heidegger's statement, for example, that the Person is outside itself in the world to mean that the Person, according to Heidegger, is *not* in itself and is *not* the world.[10] On these grounds, Sartre maintains that the transcendence (*Existenz*) of the Heideggerian Person is a possibility only because negation had already implicitly been incorporated into the structure of the Person. This negation which

[8] *EN,* pp. 28-29 (lxi).
[9] *EN,* p. 28 (lxi).
[10] *EN,* p. 54 (18).

Sartre finds implicit in the Heideggerian concept of the Person corresponds to the negation obtaining between consciousness and its object—consciousness *is not* its object.

It is in a variation on the methodical doubt of Descartes, in the fact of *questioning,* that Sartre finds the best illustration of the power of negation in human consciousness. Using an argument similar to that in his treatise on the imagination, considered in the previous chapter, in which Sartre held that imagination was possible only if consciousness were somehow able to disengage itself from the world, Sartre states in *Being and Nothingness* that

> It is accordingly important that the questioner have the permanent possibility of dissociating himself from the causal series which constitutes being. . . . the question issues forth from a questioner who motivates himself in his being as a questioner by detaching himself from being.[11]

To question is to presuppose the possibility of a negative answer, a negative answer being one in which the questioner would encounter as a result of his questioning the fact that a certain state of affairs *is not.* But how could there be an awareness of what *is not* unless the questioner were able to transcend the plenitude of Being, unless he were able to transcend the positive given contents of awareness to envisage what *is not* given to awareness in the case of a negative answer? [12] This disengagement of consciousness from Being Sartre terms *nihilation;* as in the treatise on the imagination, the power possessed by consciousness to introduce nothingness as a factor in the world is essential to consciousness. It is not a property *possessed* by consciousness, but is its very being. And again, as in the treatise on the imagination, since freedom is grounded in the power to nihilate, and since nihilation is the being of consciousness, it follows that it is also the *freedom* of consciousness. The being of consciousness is freedom.[13]

Consciousness as freedom is not only free to disengage itself from the being of what it is as consciousness, however; it is also free to *not be* its *past.* I *am* now, but I *am not* now my past. My past is *there* and I can interpret it, but, as Sartre aptly phrases the mat-

[11] *EN,* pp. 59-60 (23-24).
[12] *EN,* p. 59 (23).
[13] *EN,* p. 61 (25).

ter, in virtue of this interpretation, the past "is put out of the game." The past remains, however, peculiarly *mine* because of its original relation to my freedom; it is I who brought it into the world.[14]

With regard to the future, it can also be said that I *am not* now my future, yet the future nevertheless *is* my future. Returning to an essentially Kierkegaardian standpoint but with a Heideggerian emphasis on the cognitive significance of moods, Sartre states that in "anguish" (Sartre's equivalent to "dread") man achieves the consciousness of his freedom:

> . . . it is in anguish that freedom is in its being in *question* for itself.[15]

The point is that anguish is the consciousness of the fact that I am my own future in the mode of *not being* it;[16] as in Kierkegaard, I am aware of my future freedom (that is, my future being) as that for which I am responsible, yet which is not within my present control for the simple reason that it is a *future* possibility, not now real.

There is also a sense in which the past is relevant to the fact of anguish, for in the past I have by my actions determined what I was to be. Agreeing with Heidegger that existence (*existentia*) precedes essence,[17] Sartre asserts that man can only be what he has determined himself to be. This is the same as Kierkegaard's position on the achievement of specific determination or "essence," discussed in the first chapter of this study. But what man *has determined* himself to be, his essence, becomes a *past* fact as soon as it is achieved. Being a past fact, it is something from which consciousness disengages itself; I *am not* now my past. And as something from which I am disengaged, my essence is ineffectual with respect to determining my future conduct—a fact which is also realized in anguish.[18] An individual, having *been* heroic, has no guarantee that in the future he will not act in a cowardly manner.

To sum up the doctrine of the for-itself before moving on to a consideration of the in-itself: consciousness, the for-itself, is human reality in its being as freedom, freedom from complete immersion in that of which it is a consciousness, as well as freedom from its

[14] *EN*, p. 159 (115).
[15] *EN*, p. 66 (29). Italics mine.
[16] *EN*, p. 70 (33).
[17] Heidegger, *Sein und Zeit*, p. 43.
[18] *EN*, p. 73 (35).

past and its achieved essence. Finally, in its thrust toward the future, the for-itself perceives in anguish its future freedom as undetermined possibility. Even though it be granted that the for-itself's disengagement from causal determinants in the world constitutes the freedom of the for-itself, has not freedom itself become an essence in violation of the prescription that existence precedes essence? The answer is no, and for this reason: as noted in the discussion of freedom in the first chapter, freedom is two-fold. Freedom involves, on the one hand, an absence of external determination; but is itself, on the other hand, also an absence of determinateness. Freedom is

> . . . an existence which makes itself perpetually and which refuses to be contained in a definition.[19]

Having no essence, is freedom therefore indescribable? The answer here is again negative; for Sartre holds, as virtually any artist would, that a description need not be of an essential structure but may rather aim at an existent itself in its peculiarity.[20] In short, we do not discover phenomenologically *what it is* to be free for that would be an essential structure; we do discover *that we are free.* The ultimate existentialist paradox is that freedom is at once the essential characteristic of human reality and yet not itself an essence.

But now it should be apparent to the reader that Sartre's employment of the Heideggerian concept of being-in-the-world is "above board" *if and only if* human reality is not free, since it has been demonstrated that the freedom of the individual consists essentially in the individual's not being engaged fully in the world. Therefore, in characterizing being-in-the-world I emphasized that the description as stated obtained only with respect to the *immediate* being in a situation, only with respect to being-in-the-world as it appears, to use a term of Heidegger's, inauthentically. Sartre's equivalent to Heidegger's notion of inauthenticity is variously termed self-deception or bad-faith. The theory of self-deception, already introduced into our discussion in seminal form in the consideration of Sartre's *The Transcendence of the Ego,* presupposes for its elaboration an understanding of Sartre's doctrine of the *in-itself,* to which we now direct our attention.

[19] *EN,* p. 513 (438).
[20] *EN,* p. 514 (438).

In *The Transcendence of the Ego,* Sartre had spoken of the Ego as an object which consciousness constitutes to mask its own spontaneity from itself. Consciousness, being a pure spontaneity, has no abiding essence; it can therefore, according to Sartre, escape from the anguish that would be occasioned by its own awareness of its completely unconditioned spontaneity. Consciousness escapes this anguish by setting up an Ego, a self, which would, as an object transcendent to itself, have a stable or abiding essence. The possession of a stable essence on the part of the self would act as a mask for the spontaneity of consciousness. For example, by identifying myself (as consciousness) with an abiding self, constituted and conceived as having a certain essence which appears to determine its acts and states—energetic, ambitious, slothful, or the like—Sartre would say that I became hypnotized by this Ego which now functions as a law for my consciousness.[21] My self, in other words, appears as an object having predictable modes of behavior; it does not, however, constitute either my true reality or my essence.

The fact remains that within the natural attitude the self does appear as an object out in the world with which it is contemporaneous; in a phrase, my self appears as Heidegger's Person in his being-in-the-world. But I, as the consciousness which according to Sartre constitutes my true being, *am not* that self. That self is an object among others standing over against consciousness. It has, in Sartre's terminology, *being-in-itself*. Being-in-itself is the mode of being of the phenomenon simply as phenomenon, that is, simply as object of awareness, *transcendent* to awareness and *independent* of the meaning-constituting activities of awareness. (That Sartre views the self as constituted by consciousness yet also as an object transcendent to consciousness creates a difficulty which he does not fully resolve.) Furthermore, as already noted, since consciousness in its being *is* only insofar as it is a consciousness of something (the in-itself), it follows that the in-itself *supports* consciousness[22] and is itself not dependent on consciousness, the reverse of the idealist's position.

Although consciousness is always in principle free to disengage itself from the in-itself as, for example, in doubting, imagining, or posing a question, consciousness still cannot avoid an element of brute givenness on the part of the in-itself. For, if consciousness could avoid this sheer givenness, it could be a consciousness of

[21] *TE,* p. 101.
[22] *EN,* p. 28 (lxi).

anything whatsoever. But this last suggestion is manifestly impossible. On the contrary, it is clear that there are certain *givens,* certain *factitious* elements over which I have no control; my awareness *is not* these givens; it cannot completely separate itself from them, but they, at the same time, cannot determine my awareness.

We have already seen that Heidegger had included as one of the aspects of *being in* the world a self-encountering by which the Person's occupation of a certain *situation* in the world was revealed through the instrumentality of mood. Sartre's concept of *facticity* is a further development of this notion of one's situation. We are not simply thrown into existence *in general;* and it is our facticity which refers to all of those specificities of the existence into which we do find ourselves thrown and there abandoned: our sex, race, nationality, place in history, and bone structure, to mention but a few. (The finals in a Miss America competition can without difficulty be considered a monumental "to-do" over various aspects of the facticity of the female sex.)

Our facticity is based on what might be termed the *adhesiveness* of the in-itself. Yet facticity is not something which can be comprehended as it is *in itself,* that is, apart from its *de facto* relationship to the person. In other words, facticity has no meaning independent of the meaning which is grafted upon it by the for-itself in its capacity to constitute meanings. For example, the manuscript at which I am now working is constituted by me as *meaning* a chance to emphasize and clarify certain aspects of existentialism. My wife, however, as I hand her another thirty-eight pages of illegibly written copy, may constitute its meaning as something to be deciphered, corrected grammatically, and typed. When at a later date the manuscript is sent to the printer, the typesetter will constitute its meaning as a configuration of letters to be symmetrically arranged in type. In each case, the meaning of the being of a certain collection of sheets of paper will be overlaid on the being *in-itself* of the paper, effectively preventing a penetration to the in-itself in its "nudity." [23]

In each of these possible forms of constituting the meaning of the in-itself, there is a disengagement from the being of the in-itself on the part of the constituting consciousness. That is to say, in order to come upon the *meaning* of a particular sector of phenomenal being (as in the case of the manuscript above), it is necessary to transcend *what is,* a certain factual given, to *what is not,* a future

[23] *EN,* p. 126 (83).

state of affairs which is now signified by the in-itself at hand. Strictly speaking, it is not the in-itself which signifies, but consciousness which attributes significance to it in virtue of its (consciousness') free projection of meaning. This disengagement from what is, in order to project what is not, is, recalling a previous discussion, an example of freedom. Human action can also be seen as an exercise of freedom, for in such action consciousness transcends a present state of affairs to a desired future state of affairs (which *is not*). Were it not for the freedom of consciousness, man could not project into the future, as desirable, a state which now *is not* but which is nonetheless grounded on the present state of the in-itself. This leads us eventually back to the role of spontaneity (a freedom beyond freedom—to borrow a turn of phrase from Mr. Tillich) and a new aspect of anguish.

Sartre begins his detailed analysis of the relation between human reality (consciousness) and action by stating two of the usual definitions relevant to this problem. A *cause* is usually considered to be a reason for the act, the "ensemble of rational considerations" which justifies an act,[24] and a *motive* is a subjective state of affairs taken to have been influential in determining one way of acting rather than another.[25] An act is generally explained as having been determined by a motive when an explanation in terms of causes is not possible; for example, when in the absence of anything to be either gained or lost by performing the act in question, the act is said to have been *motivated* by impulse.[26]

These ordinary conceptions of cause and of motive are considered by Sartre inadequate to a thorough explanation of action as it is actually found in the world. In the first place, although a cause does involve an objective apprehension of a situation, this apprehension, if it be *only* a turning of one's attention toward a situation, will not yield what Sartre is willing to term a cause. Sartre's point is that a cause has to be *revealed,* and that such a revelation will take place only if the situation in question, viewed in the light of a desired end, is taken to be a genuine means toward attaining that end. For example, if a candidate for national political office belongs to a religious minority group that is the object of at least some public suspicion, he may seek to gain votes by giving the appearance

[24] *EN,* p. 522 (445-446).
[25] *EN,* p. 522 (446).
[26] *EN,* p. 522 (446).

of suffering politically because of his religious affiliation. In this case, the motive in question is a project toward a certain *end,* the winning of political office. The *cause* is the fact that both members and nonmembers of the religious group mentioned will vote for someone whom they feel is the object of discrimination because of his religious affiliation. The point is that the *cause* does not determine or even suggest the action, but is a state of affairs that comes to light only because there is a project toward a certain end on the part of the candidate.

In the second place, Sartre turns his attention to the relation between the *motive* and the *end.* Here his position is that the occurrence of a motive is not, as in the example of the political candidate, a matter contingent upon the psychological make-up of the person who experiences the motive. On the contrary, a motive is analogous to a cause in that it too is correlated with the basic project toward a specified end.[27] It is not the functioning of ambitions that makes an individual seek national political office; rather, the motive is the individual's more or less emotional apprehension of the project toward the end of achieving such office.[28]

Finally, there remains for Sartre the problem of analyzing the initial *project* itself, which project, as we have already seen, is that toward which we apprehend ourselves as being motivated. This initial project, and it is important to qualify it as *initial* since it may "include" derivative instrumental projects, is nothing but

> . . . the original rapport which the for-itself chooses with its facticity and with the world. But this original rapport is nothing other than the being-in-the-world of the for-itself in that such being-in-the-world is a choice. . . .[29]

If this initial project, which is for Sartre literally a giving character to one's being,[30] is a determination of one's being-in-the-world, it is not surprising that Sartre takes a position regarding the being of values not unlike that of Nietzsche for whom the death of God makes man alone responsible for the values with which he endows the earth.

[27] *EN,* p. 525 (449).
[28] *EN,* p. 525 (449).
[29] *EN,* p. 534 (457).
[30] *EN,* p. 520 (443).

Sartre asserts that

> . . . my freedom is the unique foundation of values and that *nothing*, absolutely nothing, justifies me in adopting this or that scale of values.[31]

Anxious about one's freedom in this respect, the individual will flee from this responsibility for values, maintaining instead that they come from God, from nature, from "my" nature, and from society. But values and transcendent ends are not prehuman; human reality

> . . . chooses them and, by this choice itself, confers on them a transcendent existence as the external limit of its projects. . . . It is thus the positing of my ultimate ends which characterizes my being and which becomes identified with the original upsurge of the freedom which is mine.[32]

In the universe pictured by Sartre, man is condemned to be free. The only limit to freedom is freedom; the only choice we cannot make is to cease being free.[33] We experience our freedom in anguish—that point occurs early in *Being and Nothingness*—but we also experience our *initial project* in anguish; it may have been other than it is.[34] Our freedom to choose, since it *is* our being, does not itself form a more fundamental structure of human reality; there is no more fundamental structure. We thus see that the initial project which at the same time determines what we are to be and what significance the world is going to have for us is *unjustifiable*.[35] The emphasis on the sheer spontaneity of consciousness as found in *The Transcendence of the Ego* and the distinction between the totality of the real and the world, as found in *The Psychology of the Imagination,* here come together in the developed form of Sartre's existentialism. Sartre, like Heidegger, defines the world in terms of a matrix of significance ultimately referred back to the being-in-the-world of the person; the major difference between the two men on this point is Sartre's underscoring of the anguished apprehension that *I* am, alone and without reason, responsible for the choice of both my being and the being of the world.[36] The slight number of

[31] *EN,* p. 76 (38).
[32] *EN,* pp. 519-520 (443).
[33] *EN,* p. 515 (439).
[34] *EN,* p. 542 (464).
[35] *EN,* p. 542 (464).
[36] *EN,* p. 77 (39).

references to Nietzsche in *Being and Nothingness* does not prevent one from seeing in that work a highly developed if somewhat extreme conception of a Nietzschean *overman* who legislates moral values and determines the significance of the world.

Furthermore there is in this context a Kierkegaardian reflection on the necessity of *renewing* my initial project. The need for such renewal springs from the groundlessness of my being as freedom.[37] Human reality is not an existent *in itself;* it demands, if it is to be an authentic human reality, a reaffirmation of that project which, having issued forth spontaneously as a freedom beyond freedom, determines the character of my being. Finally, this reaffirmation, this "constantly renewed act," Sartre identifies with the individual's existence.[38]

Do not these descriptions, with their recurring emphasis on choice, freedom, project, and renewal, appear somewhat foreign to the texture of our everyday existence? Is Sartre's phenomenology, set down as it was during the Nazi occupation of France, too much a reflection of Sartre's own tortured life and time? Can anguish be legitimately so emphasized as a ground phenomenon when, for the most part, it seldom appears to be experienced by the "normal" personality?

The answers to these questions lie in understanding fully the mechanism of self-deception, already introduced in connection with the proposed fact that consciousness avoids the anguished awareness of its spontaneity by constituting for itself a transcendent, stable Ego. Paralleling Kierkegaard's notion that the crowd is the untruth and Heidegger's conception of the inauthenticity of our everyday being-in-the-world, Sartre's theory of self-deception is perhaps the most insightful of the three in its subtle analysis of a phenomenon the existence of which cannot be denied.

The factors that enter into the mechanism of self-deception are the for-itself in its freedom and that sector of the in-itself that constitutes the facticity of the for-itself in question. The abstractness of this general statement should be clarified by the following example, which is Sartre's own; and, for those who prefer topical labels, I suggest, "How to Get Seduced without Really Trying." A woman is on a date with a man whose ultimate intentions she well understands. Since she does not, however, consider that his conduct

[37] *EN,* p. 560 (480).
[38] *EN,* p. 539 (461).

will become during the evening other than it now is, she limits her attention to his present behavior only. She avoids any sexual significance that might be *intended* by what he says by taking the immediate meaning of his words as "objective qualities."

> The man who is speaking to her seems sincere and respectful in the same way that a table is round or square, that the wallpaper is blue or grey. And the qualities thus attached to the person to whom she is listening are thus set into a thing-like permanence which is no more than the projection of their immediate present into the temporal flux.[39]

As for the woman, she is caught in a two-edged situation. She does not wish to be merely desired nor does she wish to be simply respected; the man's feelings *must be* addressed to her freedom but, at the same time, they must be projected toward her body *as object*. His desire, which she does not perceive for what it is, is taken to *mean* esteem. When he takes her hand, she is not conscious of the act for she has become "all mind." [40]

Sartre has in this example (which is repeated thousands of times weekly in the behavior of American high school and college students alone—at least, it used to be until freedom was discovered) illustrated how the ambiguity that obtains between the freedom and facticity of a person makes it possible to avoid a decision which, if directly faced, might be anguished. With respect both to her companion and herself, the woman takes the essential elements in the changing situation to be whichever ones will disarm the situation, thereby rendering it a lukewarm sequence of "interpersonal relations" (to borrow a phrase from sociology). If her companion's *intent* is to be avoided, she seizes upon the objectivity of his words. When the existence of his desire is admitted as a factor in the situation, it is blunted by referring it to her body viewed as something merely attached accidentally to herself. And when the companion takes her hand, she has but to detach herself from this advance in order to neutralize any implicit significance which that action might indicate.

It must be emphasized that the factitious aspects which constitute a virtual aura of contingency around the freedom of the for-itself do not in themselves effect the state of self-deception. It is the play

[39] *EN,* p. 94 (55).
[40] *EN,* p. 95 (55-56).

on the potential ambiguity of facticity and freedom that permits self-deception. Secondly, it is also important to note that, in spite of its role in self-deception, facticity is not good or bad in itself. For Sartre, as noted earlier, the in-itself receives its significance on the occasion of the attribution of significance to it by the for-itself which in its freedom can extricate itself from *what is* in order to project *what is not*. Finally, there is Sartre's point that the being of the in-itself is a secondary condition for freedom.

This last proposition has already been seen to be a corollary of the fact that the being of consciousness (which is freedom) depends on the in-itself as that of which the consciousness in question is a consciousness. Sartre now presents a different argument to support his contention that the in-itself is a necessary condition for freedom; namely, the very possibility of the meaningfulness of the notion of freedom (as well as of determinism and necessity) requires that the for-itself be *engaged* in a resisting world.[41] As a result, freedom is conceivable as the escape from this engagement in being. The difference between the present discussion and earlier discussions, especially in the last chapter, is that here Sartre introduces and explicates the concept of *situation* defined as the common product of freedom and the contingency of the in-itself.[42]

An example of a situation is that of *place*, a concept with which we are already acquainted in an existentialistic context in virtue of Heidegger's concern with that aspect of facticity in his reflections on self-encountering. There are, as noted, two aspects of a place as an instance of a situation. First, there is the pure contingency of the place at which I happen to be; for example, I am quite without choice an inhabitant of the mid-twentieth century. A second aspect of place, however, is that the *meaning* of my place depends on my freedom. It is in virtue of a projected future end (again, a something that *is not*) that my place in its sheer givenness (a something that *is*) receives significance. The meaning of my present place, which as a matter of fact is being at a desk in my study, is determined by the project at hand, the completion of a manuscript. But were I being held in home arrest in the same room, for example, the meaning of my place would not be a place for work but a place of confinement, a place from which I could not move. Clearly, the meaning of my place, dependent as it is on my project, is therefore dependent on

[41] *EN*, p. 561 (481).
[42] *EN*, p. 568 (488).

my choice of that project rather than some other, and this choice in turn is dependent on my initial project, that being grounded only in my spontaneity.

The reader may have noticed a similarity between this discussion and Heidegger's views on existential temporality. This is justifiable because, couched in the discussion of facticity, is Sartre's statement that the choice of the initial project regarding my being-in-the-world has a temporal dimension in that:

> . . . it makes the future come to illuminate the present and to constitute it as present by giving to the "given" in-itself the meaning of *pastness*.[43]

For example, in virtue of an initial project that defined my being-in-the-world, I choose to produce this study of existentialism. My project is a future aim toward which I now work; therefore, in the light of this aim my present place *qua* datum (the purely spatial container that is my study, the pieces of wood that are my desk and chair) is rendered *past* and is *now* constituted as *a place to work*. (One Spanish word for past, *pasado,* would suit Sartre's purposes here since it can have the connotation of *gone by and out of the way*. What my study was prior to its being constituted as *a place to work* is now *pasado*.)

Another example of a situation is *my* death; we shall consider this in the following chapter in conjunction with examining the views of Kierkegaard and Heidegger on the same topic.

[43] *EN,* p. 559 (480).

Conclusion: Death and the Existentialists

7

Nevertheless, in spite of this almost extraordinary knowledge or facility in knowledge, I can by no means regard death as something I have understood.

SÖREN KIERKEGAARD, Concluding Unscientific Postscript

Among the three existentialists with whose work we have been concerned in the course of this study, there is little agreement regarding the exact significance of death. For Kierkegaard the fact that an individual will die provides another occasion for living in his thoughts the possibility of his death—for his *becoming subjective* in the Kierkegaardian jargon. For Heidegger, death appears as a liberating goal, a *super possibility* of the Person, as it were. Finally, Sartre finds death in ultimate absurdity which, as almost everything else that Sartre takes up for consideration, leaves human freedom in its undefiled purity. However, there is one point of agreement among these thinkers when they address themselves to the problem of death: in each case the concept of death is fundamental to the existentialistic enterprises of analyzing human existence in virtue of the peculiarly intimate relation between the fact of death and human existence on the one hand, and of death and the human situation on the other.

Let me warn the reader that this discussion will not accent the morbidity of death. I do not deny that the concept of death has a morbid attractiveness about it; an article by Geoffrey Gorer is aptly entitled "The Pornography of Death." [1] But if the contributions of Kierkegaard, Heidegger, and Sartre are to be fully understood and appreciated, it is important to direct our attention away from an exclusive regard for the "pornography of death." To the extent that the "literary wing" of existentialism has, generally speaking, probably reached a larger and more interested audience than has the "technical wing," I suspect that this redirecting of attention has not too often occurred. Perhaps the present analysis may serve to lessen the role of morbidity in considering the concept of death without at the same time removing content or significance.

Of the three thinkers under consideration, Kierkegaard is the one most nearly open to the charge of morbidity, and for this reason: for Kierkegaard the uncertainty of death—that death might be "so treacherous as to come tomorrow!"—is occasion for realizing that the individual's resolve for the whole of his life must be made commensurate with that uncertainty that attends the coming of death.[2] Kierkegaard's concern is that the possibility of death does not constitute a problem of the sort that can be brought up for discussion once a year, nor, for that matter, can it be referred to committee.

My death, when it comes, will not be something in general;[3] it will not be a mere instance of dying. It is an ever-present possibility that demands my utmost concern:

> . . . and in the same degree that I become subjective, the uncertainty of death comes more and more to interpenetrate my subjectivity dialectically. It thus becomes more and more important for me to think it in connection with every factor and phase of life; for since the uncertainty is there in every moment, it can be overcome only by overcoming it in every moment.[4]

Note here that, not *the thought* of the uncertainty of death, but the uncertainty itself of death becomes involved in the subjectivity of the individual in such a way as to become an essential aspect of his existence. Stated differently, Kierkegaard treats death as constitutive of existence itself, instead of simply as the ceasing to be of existence.

For Kierkegaard there are, to be sure, questions regarding the

[1] Geoffrey Gorer, "The Pornography of Death," *Identity and Anxiety,* ed. Stein (Glencoe, Ill.: The Free Press, 1960), pp. 402-407.

[2] Kierkegaard, *CUP,* pp. 148-149.

[3] *CUP,* p. 149.

[4] *CUP,* p. 149.

meaning of death, such as whether it is possible to have an idea of death. Also, since death is a nonbeing, does it follow that death *is* only when it *is not?* Furthermore, such problems are compounded by the impossibility of the individual's experimenting with death. But all of these probings revolve around the central question of how the conception of death will transform an individual's existence in view of that individual's need to overcome the uncertainty of death at every moment.[5]

Such a need is not to be taken as a detriment to existence; to substantiate this statement we need only to recall Kierkegaard's thesis that the ethical task required of the individual is that he *become subjective.* To the extent then that the individual gives himself over to reflection on the possibility of death, he is *developing himself* in his subjectivity. The thought of death is accordingly a *thought* that is a *deed:*

> For the development of the subject consists precisely in his active interpenetration of himself by reflection concerning his own existence, so that he *really thinks* what he thinks *through making a reality of it.*[6]

There is a definite emphasis on the concept of death in Kierkegaard to the extent that the uncertainty of death thus becomes integrated into the existence of the individual. The point, as Kierkegaard notes, is not that death can be achieved by taking a dose of sulphuric acid.[7] That would be an objective consideration regarding death, not a subjective one; and Kierkegaard's concerns are emphatically confined to subjective ones. Kierkegaard in effect has, as Sartre says of Heidegger, interiorized and thereby individualized death.[8]

In his discussion of the concept of death, Heidegger does, as Sartre indicates, treat the concept in such a manner as effectively to interiorize it. Heidegger grants that the fact that "others" die makes the Person's finitude accessible.[9] Nevertheless, this indirect accessibility of the Person's finitude is neither synonymous with nor equal in significance to the answer to the question: What is the meaning of death to a Person, for whom death is a *possibility* of his

[5] *CUP,* pp. 150-151.
[6] *CUP,* p. 151. Italics mine.
[7] *CUP,* p. 147.
[8] Sartre, *L'Être et le néant,* p. 616 (532).
[9] Heidegger, *Sein und Zeit,* p. 237.

being? [10] I emphasize "possibility" in order to remind the reader of the centrality which Heidegger gives to the concept of possibility. We might recall briefly that Heidegger has characterized the Person as a being who transcends himself at once toward the world and toward his own possibilities. These possibilities, as we have noted, are not "possessions" of the Person; possibilities *have* to be chosen. And a necessary condition for this choice is the Person's understanding himself as standing out (existing) from his present self toward his future, and therefore *now* indeterminate, possibilities.

Heidegger underscores the interiority of death by pointing up that, although others can fill *my role* in life, no one can die for me.[11] Death is mine in a peculiarly intimate way which is, according to Heidegger, different in kind from the sense in which other activities are mine, since these other activities can always be performed by another who takes my place. My death could also be taken as interior to me in that it is a "not yet" which always pertains to my being;[12] that is to say, I as a Person might be viewed as a *not yet* completed totality or as something that arrives at its end. But obviously caution must be taken with this last characterization, for the Person is not a *thing* that would become a whole, for example, if it were to arrive at its end.[13] If such phrases as "not yet" and "arriving at its end" are carefully interpreted when one speaks of death, the use of such phrases is not without meaning so long as they are employed to characterize death for what it is, a mode of being assumed by the Person from the moment of his birth.[14]

With respect to the possibilities that constitute the being of the Person, death, for Heidegger, occupies a unique position in that it is the possibility of no longer being a Person.[15] Recalling that the German word which I have been translating as "Person" is literally translated as "being there," we find a stronger meaning of Heidegger's definition of death: the possibility of no longer being there (in the world). Death is also dissimilar to other possibilities of the Person in that it is unavoidable.[16]

The significance of this unavoidability of death springs from the

[10] *SZ*, p. 239.
[11] *SZ*, p. 240.
[12] *SZ*, pp. 242-243.
[13] *SZ*, p. 243.
[14] *SZ*, p. 245.
[15] *SZ*, p. 250.
[16] *SZ*, p. 250.

fact that the unavoidability of a personal possibility constitutes a curtailment of the freedom of the Person, since Heidegger has defined freedom in terms of the Person's choice of the possibilities which he is to realize. It may be because of this limiting relation imposed on human freedom by the uniqueness of death that Heidegger speaks of the Person as *thrown* into the possibility of death.[17] We have already seen in the chapter discussion of Heidegger that the notion of thrownness is allied to the self-encountering of the Person, which reveals the situation of the Person to him through moods. It appears then that death has an interestingly twofold nature in Heidegger's thought; for, as a possibility, death *is* related to human freedom, but as factitious (since thrownness is facticity), death appears as an unavoidable aspect of the Person's situation, thereby limiting human freedom.

Although death is not a possibility which the Person can refuse, Heidegger sees that for the Person there still is a dread of death corresponding to his dread of being-in-the-world. Such dread is not to be confused with fear of leaving life, for the dread of death is not a sign of weakness on the part of the Person.[18] We might also bear in mind that dread as previously considered, that is, dread *of* being-in-the-world, was conceived by Heidegger as a dread *for* being-in-the-world; dread was conceived as opening to the Person the opportunity freely to exercise his power-to-be. In brief, dread of being-in-the-world had both an occasion and an end. The dread of death has also as its end being-in-the-world; its occasion, that "about which" it is a dread, however, is simply the *power-to-be* of the Person.[19] The point here is that dread of death is more fundamental than dread of being-in-the-world. Dread of being-in-the-world is related directly to our flight before the responsibility for freely determining the *nature* of our being; dread of death, on the other hand, relates simply to our being itself. Heidegger's position here, if I have correctly interpreted it, and Hamlet's famous soliloquy are mutually reinforcing, for Hamlet's primary concern is not *how to direct his life* but *whether to live at all.* Unable to overcome the dread of being and of dying, Hamlet, it has been suggested, turns away from this primary dread and resumes the "once removed" dreadfulness of his being-in-the-world.

[17] *SZ,* p. 251.
[18] *SZ,* p. 251.
[19] *SZ,* p. 251

For the Person, his being-in-the-world in its role as the *end* of his dread of death itself receives a transformation in his reflective encounter with death. The unavoidability of death individualizes the Person. It sets him apart as *this* unique individual:

> It [also] makes it evident that all being with the object of its concerns and all being with others fails when the Person goes to his most "personal" power-to-be.[20]

This coming to naught of everyday concerns and relations with others has received, as Maurice Natanson has pointed out,[21] a classical literary statement in Tolstoy's *The Death of Iván Ilých*. During his life Iván had been the victim of a deception the cause of which had been doing as *One* does; he had taken on the values of the people whom he admired. Regarding some of Iván's sexual activities, for example, Tolstoy writes:

> It was all done with clean hands, in clean linen, with French phrases, and above all among people of the best society and consequently with the approval of people of rank.[22]

With the growing awareness of his approaching death, however, the deception is lifted:

> He [Iván] lay on his back and began to pass his life in review in quite a new way . . . In them [his footman, wife, daughter, and doctor] he saw himself—all that for which he had lived—and saw clearly that it was not real at all, but a terrible and huge deception, which had hidden both life and death.[23]

Death loses its terror for Iván when he frees himself *for* it by no longer attempting to justify his life. The transformation of Iván's attitude toward death finds a theoretical counterpart in Heidegger's statement that only the being free *for* (*towards*) death provides a goal for the Person and "pushes his existence into its finitude." [24]

[20] *SZ*, p. 263.

[21] Maurice Natanson, "Existentialism and Literature," *Reflections from Chapel Hill, I,* No. 2 (July-August 1961), pp. 3-16.

[22] Leo Tolstoy, "The Death of Iván Ilých," *Short Novels of the Masters,* ed. Neider (New York: Holt, Rinehart, & Winston, Inc., 1943), p. 258.

[23] Tolstoy, "The Death of Iván Ilých," p. 297.

[24] See footnote 72, Chapter 4.

That is, the being free for death makes possible a new aspect of transcendence on the part of the Person, a transcendence of himself to the finitude of his being, a finitude imposed by the possibility of death. Only the awareness of one's finitude extricates the Person from the endless whirl of pleasing himself, taking things lightly, and shirking tasks that fill much of everyday living.[25]

A qualified admiration for the Heideggerian conception of the meaning and role of death prefaces Sartre's reflections upon the nature of death. Especially attractive to Sartre is the philosophical sleight-of-hand by which Heidegger has attempted to disarm death as a limit of our freedom by interiorizing death.[26] Sartre here is taking aim at the difficulty which Heidegger had obscured by treating death both as a possibility of the Person *for which* he can be free, on the one hand, but also as an unavoidable possibility, on the other; that is, as a possibility that can honestly be conceived only as a limitation of the Person's freedom. Sartre uncovers the root of this Heideggerian paradox by asking whether death does belong to human reality (the Person). For if Kierkegaard and Heidegger were both wrong in considering death as a human possibility, then its occurrence in no way compromises human freedom, human freedom having been defined by our capacity to choose which of our possibilities to realize.

Sartre also finds fault with Heidegger's belief that death individualizes the Person; for on Heidegger's own terms it is the Person himself who must project himself freely toward his own death. But, if Heidegger's point be granted, then the Person is of necessity already living as an individual.[27] In fact, although *in one sense* no one else can die for me (that is, die *my* death), neither can anyone do anything else at all for me if by this we mean realize *my* possibility.[28] But if the question does not regard realizing *my* possibility, then Heidegger's point is seen to be false, for in principle another Person can always do what I do; for example, another can give his life in place of mine.

But the most important difference between Heidegger and Sartre regarding the nature of death lies in Sartre's insistence that death is not a human possibility but rather a situation which a human being must eventually confront. Heidegger was right in noting the

[25] *SZ*, p. 384.
[26] Sartre, *EN*, p. 616 (533).
[27] *EN*, pp. 617-618 (534).
[28] *EN*, p. 618 (534).

correlative status of life and death; that is, from the moment of our birth we assume death as a mode of being. But Heidegger was wrong in failing to see the *absurd* character of life and death. The absurdity of death stems from the fact that death, as Kierkegaard had most vividly portrayed it, may treacherously come *at any time*. This chance character of the moment of dying prevents it from functioning as the final chord of a melody *which emanates from the melody itself* thereby conferring aesthetic meaning upon the melody.

Death, Sartre would say, is then not a possibility of my being but an always possible *situation* involving the negation of my possibilities.[29] Were death a possibility, its being would depend on human reality just as the possibility of rain (bearing in mind that Sartre deals in phenomenology and not meteorology!) depends on my transcending the present *actual* grey clouds to the awareness of a state (rain) which now is not. Sartre holds, however, that the appearance of chance in my projects in the form of my unpredictable ceasing-to-be is sufficient evidence that death is not itself a possibility but rather a situation that negates my possibilities. It follows also that death cannot confer a meaning on life as both Tolstoy and Heidegger, each in his own way, had maintained. Only human consciousness in its freedom can constitute meaning, as we have seen in the discussion of the distinction between the pure contingency of facticity and the significance of a situation.

A further difference between death and true human possibilities is illustrated by Sartre's concept of action. In Chapter 6 it was suggested that Sartre considers action as involving the exercise of freedom in that consciousness must be able to disengage itself from a present state of affairs in order to project a desired state of affairs *in the future*. Although the future, as projected by consciousness, gives the present state of affairs a meaning as being instrumental or not with regard to the future in question, dying *has no future* open to phenomenological inspection; not having a future, it is denied the possibility of having that significance that always accrues to human action.

Indirectly, however, there is a future to *my* death, a future that is not for me but for *others*.[30] On the occasion of my death, my entire life is past. But the past is not a nonbeing; it *is*, on the contrary, in the mode of the in-itself. In and by itself the in-itself is without meaning, but the in-itself that is my past may have meaning

[29] *EN*, p. 621 (537).
[30] *EN*, pp. 624-625 (540).

bestowed upon it by other human beings who are therefore cast in the role of the guardians of my life.[31] Were it not for the existence of others, the occasion of death

> . . . would be, in effect, the simultaneous disappearance of the for-itself and of the world, of the subjective and of the objective, of the significant and of all meanings.[32]

In spite of this dreadful potential which death could in principle unlock (and may well do so *in fact,* given a successful World War III), Sartre, unlike Heidegger, conceives of death neither as a source of human finitude nor as a constraint on human freedom. That death does not constitute human finitude follows from Sartre's conception of finitude. Finitude is not a function of mortality but of freedom. In virtue of my freedom I project certain possibilities to the exclusion of others; I make myself finite by this excluding aspect of the choices by which I determine my being:

> Differently stated, human reality would remain finite even if it were immortal, because it *makes* itself finite in choosing itself as human.[33]

Neither does death serve to limit my freedom, although it is an external limit of my subjectivity.[34] Death would be such a limit were it, as conceived by Heidegger, an unavoidable possibility, a possibility which I could not refuse to choose. Sartre, however, has removed death from the realm of human possibilities. The price paid for such removal is a view of life as moving toward an absurd end; the package purchased is an uncompromising belief in human freedom as the substance of the human being.

If Sartre's conclusion here seems exaggerated, we must bear in mind that Sartre is only reasserting what Kierkegaard had first proposed: freedom is infinite. Even Sartre's self-imposed confinement of his analysis within the formalistic straitjacket of phenomenology cannot restrain completely the Kierkegaardian insistence that only decisiveness can set limits to human freedom. This last comment by no means disparages the role played by the phenomenological orientation in Sartre or, for that matter, in Heidegger. Here

[31] *EN,* p. 626 (541).
[32] *EN,* p. 630 (545).
[33] *EN,* p. 631 (546).
[34] *EN,* pp. 631-632 (547).

in the discussion of death, as elsewhere in the last three chapters, the emphasis on description which phenomenological technique entails is instrumental in providing a transition from the provocative exhortations of Kierkegaard to the systematic philosophizing of Heidegger and Sartre. The "academic" aspect given to existentialism by the Husserlian form in which it has been cast has resulted in a wider, more interested audience for Kierkegaard's insights.

The existence of such an audience, however, and the increasing sophistication of its members heighten the continuing demand for examination and constructive criticism of the Kierkegaardian tradition by philosophers sympathetic to it. Such examination serves to clarify what is essential to that tradition and what is not. Outlined in this study is an extended suggestion, a judgment, that the material here presented constitutes a case for existentialism, conceived as the exploration of the category of the individual, the category through which—". . . this age, all history, the human race as a whole, must pass."

Bibliography

Descartes, René, *A Discourse on Method and Selected Writings,* trans. Veitch. New York: E. P. Dutton & Co., 1951.

Earle, William, "Phenomenology and Existentialism," *The Journal of Philosophy,* LVII, No. 2 (January 21, 1960), pp. 75-84.

Hegel, G. W. F., *The Logic of Hegel,* trans. Wallace. London: Oxford University Press, 1950.

———, *Philosophy of Mind,* trans. Wallace. Oxford: The Clarendon Press, 1894.

———, *Selections,* ed. J. Loewenberg. New York: Charles Scribner's Sons, 1929.

Heidegger, Martin, *Existence and Being,* ed. Werner Brock. London: Vision Press Ltd., 1956.

———, *An Introduction to Metaphysics,* trans. Manheim. Garden City, N. Y.: Doubleday and Company, Inc., 1961.

———, *Sein und Zeit,* 9th edition. Tübingen: Max Niemeyer Verlag, 1960.

———, "The Way Back into the Ground of Metaphysics," *Existentialism from Dostoevsky to Sartre,* ed. Kaufmann. New York: Meridian Books, The World Publishing Company, 1951, pp. 206-221.

Husserl, Edmund, *Cartesian Meditations,* trans. Cairns. The Hague: N. V. Martinus Nijhoff's, 1960.

———, *Ideas.* London: George Allen & Unwin Ltd., 1952.

———, "Phenomenology and Anthropology," *Realism and the Background of Phenomenology,* ed. Chisholm. Glencoe, Ill.: The Free Press, 1960, pp. 129-142.

Kaufmann, Walter, *Existentialism from Dostoevsky to Sartre.* New York: Meridian Books, The World Publishing Company, 1951.

———, *From Shakespeare to Existentialism.* New York: Doubleday & Company, Inc., 1960.

———, *Nietzsche,* New York: Meridian Books, The World Publishing Company, 1956.

Kierkegaard, Sören, *The Concept of Dread,* trans. Lowrie. Princeton, N. J.: Princeton University Press, 1957.

———, *Concluding Unscientific Postscript,* trans. Swenson. Princeton, N. J.: Princeton University Press, 1944.

———, *A Kierkegaard Anthology,* ed. Bretall. New York: The Modern Library, Random House, Inc., 1946.

———, *The Point of View,* etc., trans. Lowrie. London: Oxford University Press, 1939.

———, *Sickness unto Death.* Garden City, N. Y.: Doubleday and Company, Inc., 1955.

Lowrie, Walter, *Kierkegaard.* London: Oxford University Press, 1938.

Natanson, Maurice, "Existentialism and Literature," *Reflections from Chapel Hill,* I, No. 2 (July-August 1961), pp. 3-16.

Nietzsche, Friedrich, *Beyond Good and Evil.* Chicago: Henry Regnery Co., 1955.

———, *Joyful Wisdom.* New York: Frederick Ungar Publishing Company, 1960.

———, *The Philosophy of Nietzsche,* trans. Clifton Fadiman. New York: Random House, Inc., 1937.

———, *The Portable Nietzsche,* ed. Kaufmann. New York: The Viking Press, 1960.

———, *The Will to Power,* trans. Ludovici and ed. Levy. London: George Allen & Unwin Ltd., 1924.

Ortega y Gasset, José, *What Is Philosophy?,* trans. Adams. New York: W. W. Norton & Company, Inc., 1961.

Sartre, Jean-Paul, *Being and Nothingness,* trans. Barnes. New York: The Philosophical Library, Inc., 1956.

———, *L'Être et le néant.* Paris: Librairie Gallimard, 1943.

———, "Existentialism Is a Humanism," *Existentialism from Dostoevsky to Sartre,* ed. Kaufmann. New York: Meridian Books, the World Publishing Company, 1951, pp. 287-311.

———, *The Psychology of the Imagination.* New York: The Philosophical Library, Inc., 1946.

———, *The Transcendence of the Ego,* trans. Williams and Kirkpatrick. New York: The Noonday Press, 1937.

Spiegelberg, Herbert, "Husserl's Phenomenology and Existentialism," *The Journal of Philosophy,* LVII, No. 2 (January 21, 1960), pp. 62-74.

Index